PENGUIN BOOKS

Why We Act Like Canadians

Pierre Berton's roots go deep into his country's past. The ancestor for whom he is named, Pierre Berthon de Marigny, was driven from France in the seventeenth century for his Huguenot beliefs and settled in colonial America. His great-great-great grandfather, Captain Peter Berton, brought a shipload of Loyalists to New Brunswick in 1784. His father followed the gold rush trail to the Klondike in 1898. His maternal grandfather, Phillips Thompson, was one of the best-known journalists and public speakers in nineteenth-century Ontario, an associate editor of *Grip*, a foreign correspondent for the Toronto *Globe*, and the author of the recently re-published *The Politics of Labor*, the first socialist book to be issued in Canada. The author's mother, Laura Beatrice Berton, has told her own story in *I Married the Klondike*.

The holder of three Governor General's Awards for non-fiction, Pierre Berton is a companion of the Order of Canada. The father of eight children, he has made his home in Kleinburg, Ontario, for the past thirty-seven years.

PIERRE BERTON

Why We Act Like Canadians

A personal exploration of our national character

A Penguin Books Canada/McClelland and Stewart Book

Penguin Books Canada Ltd., 2801 John Street, Markham, Ontario, Canada L3R 1B4
Penguin Books Ltd., Harmondsworth, Middlesex, England
Penguin Books, 40 West 23rd Street, New York, New York 10010 U.S.A.
Penguin Books Australia Ltd., Ringwood, Victoria, Australia
Penguin Books (N.Z.) Ltd., 182–190 Wairau Road, Auckland 10, New Zealand

Why We Act Like Canadians First published by McClelland and Stewart , 1982

Published in Penguin Books, 1987

Copyright ©1982 by Pierre Berton Enterprises Ltd.

Introduction to the 1987 edition, copyright ©1987 by Pierre Berton Enterprises Ltd.

All rights reserved.

Manufactured in Canada

Canadian Cataloguing in Publication Data

Berton, Pierre, 1920–
  Why we act like Canadians

ISBN 0-14-010442-9

1. Nationalism — Canada.   2. National characteristics, Canadian.   I. Title.

FC97.B47 1987   971   C87-093593-3
F1021.B47 1987

Letters to an American Friend

INTRODUCTION

The puzzle of free trade   *1*

ONE

Peace, order and strong government   *15*

TWO

Big Daddy in a scarlet coat   *31*

THREE

Once a Loyalist…   *53*

FOUR

Of kilts and babushkas   *79*

FIVE

When mercury freezes   *97*

SIX

The solemn land   *111*

Why We Act Like Canadians

INTRODUCTION
TO THE 1987 EDITION

The puzzle of
free trade

Dear Sam:

It's been awhile since you and I have exchanged letters. But now that my correspondence with you is to be published in a new edition, I really must reply to your most recent query about free trade. You sound puzzled, Sam. You tell me you haven't been able to get a handle on the free trade issue. I don't doubt it since your own newspapers haven't given much more space to the subject than they've given to trade relations with Albania.

You're puzzled, Sam? *We're* puzzled! Even if you were a constant reader of *The Globe and Mail* — the Bible of the Ottawa movers and shakers — you'd be puzzled. The whole country is puzzled because nobody, including the Prime Minister himself, knows what "free trade" actually means. In fact, the country is so much in the dark that now, at this late date, a full two years after he swept into office after embracing the free trade principle, the Prime Minister has finally realized that he must spend several million dollars "explaining" free trade to the Canadian public. First, of course, he'll have to explain it to himself. What he started out calling "free trade" was later scaled down to "freer trade" and then to "enhanced trade," or "comprehensive trading opportunities," "an equitable trading agreement," and other face-saving phrases that can mean anything or nothing and have only added to the general confusion.

In the face of a nation deeply troubled and divided over a worsening relationship with you Americans, and in the face of clear protectionist signals from your side of the border, it's no wonder Mr. Mulroney has been forced for most of his term to back and fill.

Sam, you cannot discuss free trade without discussing and examining the peculiar nature of this country — something that is discussed in the letters compiled for this book. For the free trade issue goes to the very heart of our national character. Your fellow Americans don't really understand how different we are from you. Your leadership doesn't understand it, nor does Mr. Murphy, your negotiator on the free trade issue. What distresses me is the realization that our own government doesn't appear to understand it either. The suspicion persists that Mr. Mulroney, who rose to prominence as the chief executive officer of an American-owned company, is quite prepared to bargain away some of those very aspects of our society that *make* us distinctive.

It's interesting that the one euphemism he has not used to describe his particular version of free trade is "reciprocity." Historically, that's a naughty word in Canada. As every schoolchild knows, it sunk the Liberal government of Sir Wilfrid Laurier back in 1911. Reciprocity was something very close to free trade — but not nearly as close as today in Mr. Mulroney's latest updated version.

Laurier, too, thought he had something when he came out in favour of a reciprocal trade agreement with your country but it backfired. He called an election expecting it would sweep him into office. Instead, it swept him right out, tarnishing his silver image forever.

At that time, Sam, we Canadians were in a far better bargaining position than we are today. You Americans *wanted* free trade with Canada, perhaps a little too eagerly to suit our more cautious countrymen. We admire Americans but it's a bit of a love–hate relationship. We don't like cosying up too closely. It reminds me of the time when, as an ambitious young reporter, I offered to get into the lion's cage with Clyde Beattie, their tamer. "They'd gobble you alive before you took two steps," he said. I figured it just wasn't worth the notoriety. Well, it was the same in 1911 when your speaker-designate, Champ Clark, announced he'd welcome the day "when the American flag will float over every square foot of the British-North American possessions to the North Pole." All the latent anti-Americanism that has always simmered beneath the deceptively placid surface of Canada's external relations simmered to the top. That finished Laurier politically and it killed any talk of reciprocity for half a century. We wanted "no truck nor trade with the Yankees," to quote the slogan of the day.

The suspicion that free trade means an eventual American takeover was strong then and remains strong today. It is not helped by American indifference and insensitivity to Canada's problems and Canada's interests. When *The Globe and Mail* in a lead editorial refers to "the American bully," as it did when discussing the negotiations over the proposed U.S. tariff on softwoods, it tells you something about the depth of Canadian feeling. For the *Globe* has generally been a proponent of a free trade agreement.

The free trade debate also tells you something about the state of political philosophy in this country: there isn't any. Take my own case. I have, on occasion, been asked to run for public office by all three major parties, none of whom appeared to give a hoot where I stood on any issue. "I'm not a Liberal," I tried to explain to Keith Davey when he invited me into the fold. "That doesn't matter a bit," he said cheerfully. "I think I can forecast that you'll be in the Cabinet." Look at Mulroney. In seizing what he once thought was a popular issue, he chucked a century of Conservative philosophy out the window and convinced his followers to perform a political arabesque, whirling tradition about in a one-hundred-and-eighty-degree turn that must have caused the Father of our Country to perform a similar revolution in his tomb.

For it is traditionally the Liberals and not the Tories who have cosied up to the Yanks. They were the continentalists; the Conservatives, the Chinese wall protectionists. After all, our first prime minister, John A. Macdonald, was able to roar back into office after the greatest political scandal of the century on the strength of his "National Policy." Macdonald, the high tariff Tory, launched and then propped up the tottering Canadian Pacific Railway to prevent the American expansionists from grabbing the Canadian West. No free trade for him.

See him now, Sam, on that memorable December day in 1880. He is old and tired, his face veined from too much gin and too much port, but pale now from a crippling stomach ailment that makes it all but impossible for him to stand. Yet stand he does for more than three hours, delivering the finest speech of his career, hammering home the adverbs as he cries out that the railway will be built, "vigorously, continuously, systematically and successfully!" It will be an all-Canadian line "which will give us a great and united, rich and improving, developing Canada, instead of making us tributary to American bondage, to American tolls, to American freights, to all the little tricks and big tricks that the American railways are addicted to for the purpose of destroying our road." This is vintage Macdonald, the bold rhetoric that turned him into a Canadian icon.

The railway would open the West and supply the West with manufactured goods from the East — goods whose high price tag was made possible by the tariff on competing American profits. No wonder, then, that traditionally, Western Canada has been for free trade while Eastern Canada has opted for protection.

But that's all in the past. When Mulroney, flushed with a massive electoral victory, made free trade the main thrust of his new government, the country responded with enthusiasm. *Wow!* More jobs! Lower prices on imported American goods! Cheaper TV sets, stereos, wine, shoes, even automobiles! No more lining up at customs counters; no more shabby attempts at smuggling; no more petty irritations from petty officials! It sounded too good to be true and it was.

In the past couple of years, Sam, support for free trade in Canada has been eroded steadily as Canadians come to grips with the realities of Mulroney's grand design. Today, close to half the population is opposed or lukewarm. For when the chips are down, we Canadians have always been willing to pay a price for living in this small, peaceable kingdom. And the price is beginning to look pretty high. We got a hint of it the other day during the negotiations over the export of Canadian softwoods. Fine. That meant money in the government coffers. But you Americans made one thing clear. We can't use a nickel of that money to help prop up those smaller lumber firms who will be hit hardest by the new price structure.

Subsidy. That's a great Canadian word, Sam, but

it's anathema to American businesses that want to compete in Canada. In this country we subsidize everything from Atlantic fishermen to prairie farmers, from book publishers to aircraft companies. The shape and nature of the country demand that the strong prop up the weak. That philosophy is so deeply ingrained in the Canadian tradition that it's unthinkable to abandon it. Yet that's what your business community would like us to do. To them, the social, cultural and economic net that we have so laboriously woven to protect our identity simply boils down to unfair trade practices. Unemployment insurance? Medicare? Family allowances? Why, you say, these are subsidies that allow you Canadians to compete unfairly in the wage and salary market.

As for culture — we don't even speak the same language. You think of culture in terms of opera, ballet and classical music. To us it covers everything from Stompin' Tom Connors to Hockey Night in Canada. What is merely "industry" to you is culture to us. Books, movies, radio, television — all culture. Anne Murray is culture. Wayne and Shuster are culture. *Maclean's* magazine is culture. Farley Mowat is culture. The government subsidizes them all, in one way or another, because all are genuine Canadian artefacts, distinct and unique, something we have that nobody else has — the ingredients of our national mucilage.

Your businessmen don't understand this, nor do your politicians and diplomats. It baffles and irks them.

Why, they ask, should Canadian radio stations be forced to play so much Canadian music? Why should Canadian advertisers be penalized if they want to use American border television stations? What's all this nonsense about film quotas? Why can't *Time* magazine publish a Canadian edition without the government setting out the rules? To us Canadians this is a necessary form of cultural protectionism; to those of you who think of Canada as another state in the union — part of the American domestic market — it's unfair competition.

Not long ago, your newest ambassador to our country, discussing this question of cultural sovereignty, made a remark about television so appalling in its ignorance that one wondered what flat stone he'd been languishing under. He said he couldn't understand why we Canadians were so steamed up about the predominance of American programs on our networks. Why, said he, PBS network in the U.S. was loaded with British imports but his countrymen weren't a bit concerned about this threat to their sovereignty! This remark went unchallenged in Canada, probably because the idea of American culture being threatened by Masterpiece Theatre was so ludicrous that it didn't require comment. But if one of your leading diplomats is so myopic, what hope has our negotiating team got in Washington?

The letters in this book, Sam, were written to make it clear to Americans and Canadians that we are two different peoples: we run our country in a different fashion than you do, not necessarily better and not necessarily worse, but in our own way — a way that happens to fit our peculiar environmental, cultural, economic and historic background. Can we hang on to this Canadian way and still enjoy the advantages of free trade? That's what the discussion is all about.

Many of us have reservations. It may well be true that a "comprehensive trade agreement" will produce more jobs for Canadians. But you don't get something for nothing at the bargaining table. Trade agreements involve trade-offs. No one knows what our government is prepared to give away, but everyone who's read his history knows that you Americans have an enviable record of horse trading and wheeling and dealing. You're good at it. We're not, as history also shows.

At the turn of the century we got the short end of the stick in negotiations over the Alaska boundary. As a result we've been denied a saltwater port on the part of British Columbia that is blocked by the Alaska panhandle. In 1947, a group of Hollywood sharpies came up to Ottawa and convinced the Canadian government to scrap its plans for a film quota. Ever since then almost every nickel made at a Canadian box office by an American movie has gone back to the United States. Had the government insisted that some of it be invested here we might now have a thriving film industry. And then in the 1950s, in spite of the valiant efforts of Andy McNaughton, we handed you Columbia River power on a platter. British Columbia has been trying to get it back ever since. In the light of these past follies it's hard to see how we can come out of the current discussions without surrendering some of those peculiar institutions and practices that help make us a distinct and sovereign people. Not everybody in Canada worries about this, Sam; but it's this fear that's at the basis of the free trade debate that puzzles you so much.

And that, of course, is the kicker. In the end the discussion about free trade may be seen as more important than free trade itself. All unwittingly, Mr. Mulroney has plunged this country into a full scale debate about the nature of Canada and its institutions. For the first time, Canadians have had to ask themselves what kind of people we are and what kind of people we want to be. How important is this network of support we've fashioned for ourselves? What parts of it are we prepared to give up? What will we insist on keeping no matter what the cost? The marathon argument over reciprocity, which some have seen as divisive, has actually drawn us together as a people. It's been a learning experience for everybody: for the pundits and the labour leaders, for the businessmen and the blue-collar workers, for the scribblers and the politicians.

It's also been a learning experience, I suggest, for the Right Honourable Brian Mulroney.

March 1, 1987

ONE

Peace, order and strong government

---

*In Canada you are
reminded of the government every day.
It parades itself before you.
It is
not content to be the servant, but will
be the master....*

HENRY DAVID THOREAU, 1866

*D*ear Sam:

Today is Constitution Day in Canada! That doesn't mean much to you, I know — I doubt if it will make your front pages — but it's a big thing for us. After centuries we've cut our last ties with Europe and we're officially independent; our Queen says so. In fact she's up there on Parliament Hill, saying it now with a very English accent. But then we're used to English accents in this country — to a babel of accents: English, French, Scottish, Irish, Ukrainian, Italian, and many, many others — symbolizing those fierce ethnic and regional loyalties that hold us together as a distinctive people even as they tear us apart. A typically Canadian contradiction.

Up on Parliament Hill they're singing "O Canada"

in two languages and more than one version. They're also singing "God Save the Queen," because, you see, we still have a Queen and she's all ours, even if she drops in on us only occasionally from her home at Buckingham Palace. By another typically Canadian contradiction we have been made to believe that she is not the Queen of England, except when she's in England, but the Queen of Canada, even when she's not here. That allows us to be totally independent on this day of days: an odd business, when you think of it, since we have been insisting to you Americans for decades that we've really been independent all along.

But then, we were only acting like Canadians, confusing everybody, especially your countrymen, who can't see much difference between our two peoples.

I know you're confused yourself, because every time you visit this country you ask questions which indicate to us that we *are* a different people:

You want to know why you can't buy a six-pack in a Toronto deli. And why does the West hate the East? And why do some people wear kilts at parties? And why are our streets safer than yours? And why did we let the Mounties get away with all those crimes? Why do people call Trudeau a pinko? What are family allowances? Why have we got movie censors? How come there are no English signs in Montreal? Why don't our newspapers carry scandal columns? How come we mispronounce "about"? What does Precambrian mean? Why are our bankers so secure and also so cautious? What's a crown corporation? How come nobody owns a gun? Why didn't we have a revolution, like everybody else? Why don't we join up with the United States?

That last question is one you've asked more than once and it deserves an answer. The short answer is that we wouldn't mind, but only if you'd let us call the country Canada and retain the parliamentary system of government, along with our flag, anthem and official bilingual policy. I doubt if you'd go for that; and even if you did it wouldn't work. We really are quite different from you Americans, even though we talk and dress and look alike.

We *have* a distinct identity and your question requires a longer answer than the flippant one I just gave. I've been exploring that identity for most of my career. And now, on this damp April day, as Mr. Trudeau pops up on the tube sounding not the slightest bit pinkish, I'm going to borrow from my own researches into the epic moments of our past, and also from my travels from Nanaimo to St. Anthony, to try to explain, in a series of letters, why we act like Canadians.

I'm going back, first, to my own beginnings because that's where I originally began to see that our social attitudes were not the same as yours.

As you know, I was born and raised in the Yukon. My father left New Brunswick at the height of the Klondike gold rush, took advantage of a railway rate war, climbed the Chilkoot Pass, built a raft on the shores of Lake Bennett, and in the spring of 1898 floated down the Yukon River to Dawson City. He didn't talk much about those days, though I still remember his description of that long line of men on the Chilkoot — a human garland hanging across the chill face of the pass — so tightly packed that, when an exhausted climber stepped out of line it took him hours to squeeze back in, cursing and hollering over the delay. He told me something else that I've never forgotten. He said that on the Canadian side of the border a man could lay down his pack, or even a sack of gold, in the middle of the trail and return for it in a week, knowing no one would touch it; such was the state of the law in the Canadian Yukon.

I know that many of your countrymen think the Klondike is part of Alaska and that it was once a wild and lawless place. What my father was trying to tell me was that, because of the Canadian passion for order and security, it was just the opposite.

I don't think I entirely believed him then. The silent films about the great stampede that Fred Elliott showed in his movie house in Dawson suggested the opposite. And I remember wondering, as a child, why *anybody* would want to leave a sack of gold lying around. But many years later, while digging into the history of the gold rush, I came upon an actual incident that suggested my father was not exaggerating. Let me set the scene for you:

The richest man in the Klondike was Big Alex McDonald, a huge, awkward prospector from Antigonish, Nova Scotia. He was so wealthy that he kept a bowl of nuggets on a shelf in his cabin to give away to visitors. His string of mules, each loaded with a hundred-pound sack of gold, was a familiar sight, moving in single file from his claim on Eldorado creek to the bank in Dawson City. One day, one of these mules broke away from the string, strayed into the hills and didn't turn up in Dawson for a fortnight.

This errant animal, stumbling about through the birches and aspens, brushing past trappers' cabins and prospectors' tents, stands for me as a symbol of Canadian probity. For it must have been seen and recognized by scores of men who had come to the north hoping to find a fortune. On its back, for the taking, was a treasure worth twenty thousand dollars. Yet nobody touched it: Big Alex got his mule back with the gold intact.

Let me remind you that in those days Dawson was really an American town on Canadian soil. Its population was at least three-quarters foreign. But nobody dared tangle with the Canadian concept of order and security.

This very Canadian mule illustrates our national preoccupation with peace, order and good government — by which, I must tell you, we Canadians generally mean "strong government." I'm afraid that those sturdy Canadian words, inscribed on parchment by the men we call the Fathers of Confederation, lack both the panache and the hedonism of the companion phrase in your own eloquent Declaration of Independence. But I must tell you, Sam, that life, liberty and the pursuit of happiness are lesser Canadian ideals. "Liberty" sounds awkward on the Canadian tongue; we use "freedom," a more passive-sounding word. When I was a soldier applying for a three-day pass, I asked for "leave," a word that suggests permission. Your G.I.s were granted "liberty," a word that implies escape.

But then, we were never a community of rebels, escaping from the clutches of a foreign monarch. For many decades, while you were entrenching, often through violence, the liberty of the individual to do his own thing, we remained a society of colonials. Basking in the security and paternalism that our constitutional phraseology suggests, we sought gradually and through a minimum of bloodshed to achieve our own form of independence.

To realize what we consider to be the best of all possible worlds, we Canadians have been prepared to pay a price. The other side of the coin of order and security is authority. We've always accepted more governmental control over our lives than you have — and fewer civil liberties.

But you, too, have paid a price. For the other side of the coin of liberty is licence and sometimes anarchy. It seems to many of us that you Americans have been willing to suffer more violence in your lives than we have for the sake of individual freedom.

When my fellow Canadians say that their own history is dull, they really mean that it does not follow the American model. We do have our own fascinating epics; I have written about some of them. But to many

Canadians, nurtured on tales of revolution, civil war and the wild west, these relatively bloodless dramas are not "history."

I think we are all fascinated by the length of your ballot — all those judges, district attorneys, police commissioners and other petty officials standing (or, as you would say, *running*) for public office. Your kind of democracy sprouts upwards from the grass; ours is dispensed from the heavens, like gentle rain. The idea of *electing* a policeman is foreign to us. I, for one, am fascinated by the notorious gunfight at the O.K. Corral, one of your sturdiest western myths. Hollywood has made at least six major pictures about that brief encounter in Tombstone. Yet none has made the real point: that it was, in many ways, a *political* battle between Wyatt Earp, who was running for county sheriff, and the forces of his political opponent, the incumbent, Johnny Behan. Gunfights of all kinds are foreign to the Canadian experience but gunfights between political policemen are as strange to us as the blood feuds of the Montagues and the Capulets.

I want to take you back to the Klondike trails, Sam, not only because that is my country, both geographically and historically, but also because it is the one place and the one time when it is possible to view both our peoples in the mass, struggling along, side by side, heads bowed, packs bulging, crossing and recrossing the international border between Canada and Alaska.

If you climb the passes with me you will notice a basic difference in attitudes toward authority. On the Canadian side, the Canadians do as they are told — and the Americans too, albeit grudgingly, if they want to stay in the country. On the Alaska side, the Americans do as they please until rules are needed; then they form a committee, elect a chairman and abide by the decisions of the majority.

You will know from your own history that this is a very American form of on-the-spot democracy. It goes back, in fact, to the New England town meeting. On the mining frontier, from California to Circle City, Alaska, the prospectors ran their own affairs through the similar device of the miners' meeting.

Let us look in briefly on a miners' meeting in Oscar Ashby's log saloon in Circle City, *circa* 1895. The town has no jail, courthouse, lawyers, sheriff, post office or bank. But here in this dark, smoky barroom, lit only by candles and furnished with rough lumber, the miners are making their own law.

This is the ultimate tribunal. It can, and has, hanged men, lashed them, banished them — but only when one man's freedom of action has threatened another's. Here now is a saloonkeeper, charged with seducing a girl of mixed blood. One of the miners has called the meeting, as is his due; all have the right to examine witnesses — and they're using it. Each man can act as prosecutor, defence counsel and juror. The verdict, by a majority vote, is guilty: the accused man must marry the girl or spend a year in a jail which, the meeting decrees, will be built especially to hold him. Fortunately, the miners are saved this labour when the prisoner opts for a shotgun wedding.

This is a marvellous little scene, Sam: justice dispensed with the wisdom of a Solomon at the grass-roots level. But I must tell you that all the miners' meetings were not so even-handed. At worst, the device was merely an extension of the vigilante movement that also had its birth in California. For the rule of the majority can also degenerate into the tyranny of the majority and that is what happened in both Circle City and Fortymile, the Yukon River community populated almost entirely by Americans but on the Canadian side of the international border. Here liberty degenerated into licence.

Now, let's look at the way in which our two governments dealt with the institution of the miners' meeting.

In Circle City, U.S.A., a bartender named Jim Chronister shot a gunfighter to death in his saloon, then offered himself up to the judgment of a miners' meeting and was acquitted in just twenty minutes on the grounds of self-defence. The verdict was sent to Washington and confirmed, thus giving quasi-official status to the miners' court.

In Fortymile, Canada, a local trader, John Healy, complained to Ottawa about the tyranny of the miners' meeting and the Anglican bishop, William Bompas, reported that the miners were feeding the Indians liquor and indulging in gunplay in the saloons. The Canadian government immediately dispatched a force of North West Mounted Police to the scene; the institution of the miners' meeting was abolished; peace, order and strong government reigned.

Now, as you know, the Americans who toiled over the passes were not prospectors. Most of them were blue- and white-collar workers from the cities. The tradition of the miners' meeting was not known to them. Nonetheless, in Alaska, they slipped easily into the American practice of rule by committee. It seems to have been second nature to them, just as it was second nature to the Canadians on their side of the border to accept the rule of authority.

Stand with me, in the snow and mud of Sheep Camp at the foot of the Chilkoot on February 15, 1898. In one of these hastily erected sheds, amid the flicker of smoking oil lamps and candles, a committee of stampeders has just sentenced a thief named Hansen to fifty lashes and now, as the crowd howls for blood, the same committee appoints a man to carry out the sentence. This is but one of many instances when, on the American side, a committee was formed to make the law — or break it. At Circle City, a committee of miners actually held up a steamboat at rifle point and unloaded thirty tons of food, because the town was starving. At Rampart, another Alaskan town, another committee, again faced with starvation, broke open a warehouse and when a U.S. infantry officer tried to arrest the ringleader, the same committee broke open the jail and freed him.

I want to make two points here. The American tradition of taking the law into one's own hands is deeply ingrained, but in neither case did the miners consider they were breaking the law; they were *making* it. Their chief concern was not for private property but for the public good. But it is also true that in Rampart, and elsewhere, liberty came perilously close to licence. The attack on the warehouse degenerated into looting: six thousand ounces of gold dust were stolen as well as the needed food.

The Canadian town of Dawson was also starving that winter but there was no looting, no extra-legal action. Charles Constantine, the burly Mounted Police inspector in charge, staved off panic by handing out free steamboat passes and five days' supply of food to anyone who would leave town. Scores did; peace and order prevailed. Constantine, too, made up the law on the spot for the sake of the public good. But this was law handed down on high by a government appointee, in the Canadian fashion.

The Klondike stampede was the only *organized* gold rush in history. The police shepherded more than seven thousand home-made boats down the Yukon River in the spring of 1898, guiding them through lakes, canyon and rapids for five hundred miles as if they were escorting a naval armada. And when the Americans started to drown themselves in Miles Canyon, as, apparently, they considered they had a perfect right to do, the authorities put a stop to it.

"There are many of your countrymen who have said that the Mounted Police make the laws as they go along," is the way the Mountie Superintendent, Sam Steele, phrased it, "and I am going to do so now *for your own good.*" The italics are mine; they underline the Canadian philosophy.

In the Yukon, the police actually banished people for serious offences. This extra-legal authority was remarkably effective since nobody wanted to be forcibly ejected from the area they had struggled so hard to reach. Thus the Canadian authorities had no trouble bringing peace and order to what might have been a rip-roaring town. For I must point out that Dawson was heavily American. Western gunfighters like Buckskin Frank Leslie rubbed shoulders with western gun molls like Calamity Jane. These old frontiersmen sometimes talked big but in practice acted as tamely as any Canadian.

I love the story of the Dodge City gunfighter, bounced from a Dawson saloon for "talking too loudly." There's a Canadian offence for you. Can you imagine Doc Holliday being thrown out of the Long Branch saloon for raising his voice? There was, in this case, a further humiliation. The gunfighter had his gun and, in Dawson, that was a serious offence. As soon as the Dodge City cowboy landed on the street a beardless Mountie constable approached and asked him to hand over the illegal weapon. A piece of Hollywood dialogue followed.

Gunman: No man has yet taken a gun away from me!

Mountie: Well, I'm taking it.

At this point his opponent understood that he was no longer in Dodge City and the young constable was not a lone marshal. The Mountie was not part of a democratic popularity contest; he did not have to appear before the electors to justify his conduct. He did not even need to be quick on the trigger because he depended for his authority on the sure knowledge that no matter what happened to him personally, another man in a scarlet coat would take his place...and another and another and another. So the man from Dodge City handed over his weapon as meekly as a lamb.

The Americans were astonished by this Canadian attitude to guns and gunfighting. One warned his fellow countrymen that "you can call the toughest gambler in town anything you wish or slap him on the wrist and all he can do is sue you for slander or have you arrested for assault. But he will do nothing for himself. If you get in trouble call a policeman. The old American stall of self-defense just doesn't go."

Since the days of George III, Americans have resisted authority; Canadians, by and large, have not. And it seems to me that if Canadians from time to time have endured too much authority, you Americans have suffered from too little. If government becomes too strong, it becomes arbitrary; if it becomes too weak it can also become corrupt. As one western American remarked during our first big immigration wave to the prairies, "Here you can't grease the sheriff's paw."

If there ever was a perfect example of that thesis, Sam, it's to be found in Skagway, Alaska — the kind of wide-open gold rush community we've seen in half a hundred Hollywood westerns. The town was the creature of a committee, elected by the new arrivals who set up a form of local government.

But the rule of committee quickly broke down. A confidence man, Jefferson Randolph "Soapy" Smith, moved in and corrupted the local government. The pursuit of happiness continued, twenty-four hours a day, as saloons, gaming houses and dance halls ran wide open. But no one would care to lay a sack of gold down on the streets of Skagway for as much as five seconds. In fact it was difficult to get the gold through town without it being hijacked. Skagway, in the words of Sam Steele, was "a hell on earth."

This is all old stuff, Sam, and we've seen it all in the movies: the corrupt gang running the community, the lone marshal fighting back. Except in this case, the lone marshal was a creature of the corrupt gang. Nor could Smith's corrupt gang find refuge across the border since Steele and his men had no intention of letting them into the Yukon. Those who tried to sneak across were quickly frog-marched back by a red-coated sergeant. This was certainly not democracy; order was achieved at the expense of human rights. The Mounted Police decided on the spot who would and who would not be allowed to continue on to the city of gold.

If the Canadians dealt with miscreants in their own fashion, so did your countrymen, Sam. As usual, they did it by electing a committee and Soapy Smith died in a gunfight at the hands of its representative.

That could not have happened in Canada. In the Yukon, as in the earlier British Columbia mining camps, we had no committee meetings, no vigilante groups, no handguns. The territory was run by a small force of men in buffalo robes — a colonial constabulary. To the Mounted Police, liberty was secondary to order; the pursuit of happiness was not as vital as the pursuit of peace and security. The Americans might complain, but the Canadians wanted it that way and still want it that way. In my country, the Mountie image is sacrosanct and the odd thing is, my friend, that you Americans helped to invent it.

TWO

Big Daddy in a scarlet coat

*The Police
have protected us as the feathers
of the bird protect it from
the frosts of winter*

CROWFOOT, BLACKFOOT CHIEF, 1877

*D*ear Sam:

Today is a holiday — the Queen's birthday — and I'm having a party to celebrate it. It seems a good day, too, to respond to the puzzlement that my last letter clearly caused you. The Queen we're honouring today, incidentally, is not the new Queen, Elizabeth — we don't get a holiday on *her* birthday — but the old Queen, Victoria, dead now for more than eighty years. Old habits, old customs and, as I am trying to show in these letters, old attitudes are hard to erase. The government is spending millions trying to get us to shoot off fireworks on July 1, the anniversary of Confederation. They're even forcing $60,000 worth of fireworks on Yellowknife, which doesn't want them because at that time of year the subarctic sky is brighter than a Roman candle. But almost everybody I know still puts punk to pinwheel on the anniversary of the old Queen's birth; and still insists on calling July 1 "Dominion Day," even though the government is trying to get us all to call it "Canada Day." We are creatures of habit, we Canadians.

You are clearly confused by the concluding sentence in my last letter. But I didn't say you Americans invented the Mounties; I said you invented the *image*. As a result, we Canadians are almost as awestruck by the Mountie myth as you are. In fact, it's partly *because* you revere our Mounties that we also revere them; after all, the Mounties are something we've got that you haven't.

You can't begin to understand us until you've examined our national icon. Because in the eyes of most Canadians, the Mountie has always been the Man Who Can Do No Wrong, even when he burns a barn or steams open our personal mail. For the Mountie is both our present-day protector and our frontier symbol, as indestructible in legend as the U.S. town marshal, his western American counterpart. Like the marshal, the Mountie myth figure is largely a Hollywood concoction. The big studios made 250 motion pictures about the force in their great days, and these films, together with novels by men like James Oliver Curwood, radio programs like "Renfrew of the Mounted," comic strips like "King of the Royal Mounted" and TV half-hours like "Sergeant Preston of the Yukon" (the latter scripts being line-by-line adaptations of "The Lone Ranger") have perpetuated the myth of the Mountie as a kind of red-coated American sheriff who always gets his man.

He wasn't and he isn't. The Mounted Policeman, in fact, is the direct antithesis of the western American lawman. Let's look at the two as they stride into our ken.

Here comes Bat Masterson or Wild Bill Hickok or Wyatt Earp. These men, technically at least, are servants of the people, elected by popular suffrage, dependent for their authority on the will of the community. Often eccentrically dressed — Earp in a long frock coat, Masterson in a bowler — they are heavily mustached, usually unshaven, shaggy-maned, and rumpled. Hollywood tended to clean up the image, but the essential truth shows through the costume department's beautifully stitched shirts and freshly laundered bandannas. These men are individuals — saloonkeeper or gambler one day (as Wyatt Earp was), lawman the next — a quirky, unpredictable breed, often enough shooting first and asking questions later.

Now here comes the Mountie, cantering to the tune of "Bonnie Dundee," immaculate and to a large extent faceless, a spit-and-polish cog in a military machine, resplendent in the Queen's scarlet, his riding boots boned to a high lustre, his spurs sparkling. If the American represents individualism — the right to choose your own freewheeling protector — the Mountie represents order and authority — the right to have your protector chosen for you. He must be seen to be impeccable. I think my most intriguing vision, taken from western Canadian history, is that of the young constables at Fort Walsh, in the heart of the Blackfoot country, being carried feet first onto the parade square to avoid the scandal of uncreased trousers. No Hollywood movie could equal that scene.

The frontier Mountie was actually a soldier, disguised as a policeman by a shrewd prime minister who didn't want to annoy you Americans; had soldiers chased the whiskey traders back to Montana it might have been considered an act of war. But the Mountie quickly became more than a soldier. Over the years he took his place as a father figure in a nation that adores father figures. Incorruptible, adaptable, courageous, courteous, kind (he had all the Boy Scout virtues, as well as the hat), the Mountie's comforting presence prevented our west from going wild. The Indians called him "father" to his face, but it was not only the Indians who appreciated his paternal qualities.

Since you are familiar only with movie Mounties, Sam, it may surprise you to learn that the North West Mounted were created not to save the white men from the wild Indians but to save the Indians from the wild white men. These wild men were mostly Americans — wolf hunters and whiskey peddlers, whose log forts bore such names as Whoop-Up, Stand-Off, and Robbers' Roost that more than hint at the state of society in what is now southern Alberta. This was the American west transferred to Canada; the Mounties were invented specifically to put an end to it.

The potent brew dispatched to the natives in exchange for furs packed such a wallop that your fellow countrymen passed it out in tin cups through a slit in the logs rather than face the blood fury of the Blackfoot braves, driven to manic lengths by a satanic concoction of straight alcohol, Perry Davis painkiller, red ink, Castile soap, Hostetter's Bitters, blackstrap molasses and chewing tobacco. A massacre of some sort was inevitable; but in the Cypress Hills, Sam, it was the Indians who were massacred by your people, who believed the only good redskin was a dead one.

Before I get to the massacre, I have to tell you something about our attitude to the native peoples of my country. In recent years, it has been mainly one of indifference. We have certainly been callous about our Indians but we have not been genocidal. We have no Wounded Knees in our history, no Little Big Horns, either. We don't boast too much about this because everyone knows our treatment of the Indians was a matter of mercantile self-interest. We used the Indian as a servant to help harvest a rich trove of furs; it made sense to look after him.

Sex also entered into the picture. In an all-male white society, the Indian women were almost as valuable as the male hunters and trappers. As the remarkable Chipewyan chief Matonabbee told the explorer Samuel Hearne, they not only pitched tents and mended clothing, they also kept the men warm at night. The Hudson's Bay Company, the first of several paternalistic institutions that have shaped our national attitudes, made certain that these women and their off-spring were properly treated. We must also give the fur traders their due: they married their native consorts, raised their half-caste children, and often gave them as good an education as the all-white sons of other Canadians.

Nor was the Indian a threat to western expansion as he was seen to be in your country. The way to the west was barred by geography not by humans. Therefore the Indian fighter is as foreign to our experience as the fighting Indian. Save for one fleeting explosive moment in 1885 when the Crees rose briefly and vainly, we have nothing to compare with Cochise, Geronimo, Sitting Bull or all the other valiant native leaders who form part of your national tradition.

The Cypress Hills massacre was an American aberration on Canadian soil. A party of Montana wolf hunters, believing their horses to be stolen by a marauding Indian band, rode two hundred miles into Canadian territory and, in a pitched battle, slaughtered some two dozen Assiniboine Indians. This was too much for the Canadian government. The prime minister rose in the House of Commons to denounce "whiskey-sodden American brigands" and shortly afterward a military expedition disguised as a police force was sent west to bring peace, order and strong government to our prairie country.

The Americans made large threats, but before the men in scarlet tunics and pillbox hats arrived in a column three miles long, the whiskey peddlers and wolf hunters had quit their forts and high-tailed it across the border. A new fort soon replaced Whoop-Up. With its scrubbed barrack-rooms and white-washed palisades, it stood as a symbol of austere Canadian authority in the wilderness.

And so, Sam, we had no wild west. You couldn't even buy a drink on the prairies. Here's a description of Medicine Hat in 1883 taken from the memoirs of a railway land examiner: "It was a rough place then . . . . Miners, cowboys, trappers, prospectors gathered in the saloons *to drink soft drinks* and play cards." Again, my italics underline the Canadian attitude: that booze is sin. We pretended we were protecting the Indians. We were also, in our Calvinistic way, speeding the construction of the railway. Drink brings sloth and that is wicked. We banned the Blackfoot Sun Dance for similar reasons, not really because of the pain suffered by the young braves but because it gave the natives an excuse to stop tilling the soil on the reserves. Every province, Sam, has a Liquor *Control* Board that controls price and distribution. But we like to think it saves us from the devil.

Our Mounties were really civil servants and social workers, enforcing the blue laws, succouring the sick, feeding starving Indians, settling domestic disputes, putting out prairie fires, collecting taxes, rounding up stray cattle, and taking off behind dog sleds or on horseback on endless patrols through wild, empty country.

It was dull, lonely work, scarcely the stuff from which Zane Grey novels were fashioned. The Mounted

Policeman was a diplomat, not a gunfighter. His job required tact, patience, physical stamina, flexibility and compassion; occasionally it also required raw courage. My earliest memory of the Mounties was the spectacle of Sergeant Cronkhite of the Dawson detachment coming into town after subduing a mad miner who had tried to kill him. It was Cronkhite's job to wrestle him into a strait jacket for his own protection and haul him by sledge scores of miles through the harshest terrain in the bitter cold to the town hospital.

This is all part of the Canadian pattern, Sam. For these early examples of official paternalism foreshadowed the later spectrum of social services — universal medicare, family allowances — that distinguish Canadian society today and stand out in contrast to your more individual American philosophy. In an odd way, you could say, the North West Mounted Police brought the welfare state to the frontier.

I know you were raised with a different picture of the mountie in your mind, Sam; but, then, so were many of my countrymen. Many are still confused by the image. Two royal commissions have examined certain extra-legal actions of the force and the evidence has been damning. Compared to that mild little break-in at the Watergate Hotel by a bunch of political bunglers, the Mounties' law-breaking tricks look very dirty indeed — and far more effective.

Consider this: income tax returns forged, letters faked, innocent people intimidated, mail obtained fraudulently and later destroyed, buildings burglarized and even burned; dynamite stolen; incriminating evidence planted on innocent people; wires tapped, phones bugged, left-wingers harassed. Yet no Mountie has yet gone to jail. Damaging files have vanished. Relevant evidence has been kept secret. But the Canadian public has remained relatively unmoved by all these revelations. In fact, public praise of the force by any aspiring politician is sure to bring a round of applause. We have lived too long with our national myth; we cannot bear to see it shattered.

The myth came into being as the result of two events that occurred almost simultaneously just before the turn of the century: the discovery of gold in the Klondike and the invention of the motion picture camera. Legends were already being fashioned in the West: Sam Steele putting down a riot at Beavermouth; James Walsh kicking Sitting Bull in the pants; a lone rookie constable taking over a band of murderous Crees from an entire detachment of U.S. cavalry. But it was only after the gold rush that these stories began to be told.

The gold rush saved the police. By the mid-nineties, they were regarded by our government as expensive luxuries. The West was already spanned by steel and well on the way to becoming civilized. Who needed them? By 1897, the force had been chopped from one thousand to five hundred men, and the budget cut from $500,000 to $385,000.

But the news of the gold strike changed all that. Thanks to the capriciousness of that American miners' meeting at Fortymile, the police were already on duty in the Yukon. Now our government rushed to reinforce this pioneer band. The NWMP sent their finest men north, including three future commissioners.

In the two hectic years that followed, the Mountie legend — the one you were raised on, Sam — was born. Here, for the first time, tens of thousands of Americans encountered the force just as it was beginning to adopt the familiar Stetson. More important, the Klondike was an American media event. Yellow journalism was just starting to come into its own; every major newspaper and magazine had at least one representative on the trail. Hearst rushed an entire platoon of reporters to the Klondike. The Mounties received world-wide publicity, almost all of it good, and deservedly so, for they brought order out of chaos, in the Canadian fashion.

The movie makers, however, wanted blood and thunder. By the time the production studios moved from New York to Hollywood, the movie Mountie was a fixture on the screens of the nation. Almost half the movies that Hollywood has made about my country have a Mountie as the central figure. Most others have a Mountie lurking somewhere in the background. In fact a Hollywood movie about Canada without a Mountie is almost as rare as a Canadian government tourist poster without one.

The movie Mounties could do no wrong. They were, to quote one breathless ad, "generally conceded to be the most wonderful organization of trained men in the world." Or, as a *Photoplay* reviewer put it, "all Canadian heroes belong to the Royal Mounted." Well, Sam, when a Canadian makes it in the States, we all sit up and take notice. You Americans helped convince us that the Mountie was larger than life.

Actually, I've got to confess that Canada is not a country of hero-worshippers. It's common dogma, in fact, that we have neglected many of the great figures of the past. So maybe it's typical of us that our quintessential hero should be faceless, recognizable not by his features but by his uniform, interchangeable with all his fellows. That is the way he is often portrayed on the tourist posters.

Hollywood has always seen the Mountie as a western sheriff in a scarlet coat. Movie Mounties rarely keep their pistols in their holsters; the posters and advertisements show them with blazing guns. Here's one advertising *Wildcat Trooper*, starring the cowboy actor of the twenties, Ken Maynard. Wildcat *Trooper*? The very name is un-Canadian. And look at the headline: "Fights, thrills, fast riding, gunplay!" Sam, I've read the *Constable's Manual*, the Mountie bible. The point it makes is that a Mountie *never* draws his weapon, except as a last resort. That philosophy is central to the original idea of a mounted constabulary.

Your own famous roughrider, Theodore Roosevelt, was fooled by the Mountie myth. The president ought to have known better, but he really thought the Canadian West was a wild, lawless country at a time when it was populated by stolid Slavs, well-to-do American farmers, Nordic peasants and English remittance men.

Ralph Connor, our best-selling prairie novelist, astonished T.R. by telling him he had never seen a man resist a Mounted Policeman, nor had he ever known any Mountie to pull a gun to enforce the law. Roosevelt had some difficulty absorbing that intelligence. He was equally amazed and, I suspect, more than a little chagrined when Connor, himself a clergyman, described members of the force as "dry nurses to the community," who "look after the sick, rescue men from blizzards, [and] pack in supplies for people in need." Here was a picture to baffle any red-blooded American. Yet it comes closer to the mark than the Hollywood image of a scarlet-coated law-man galloping across the plains on a black charger, guns blazing.

For guns have played a minor role in our past. That's another reason why Canadians say our history is dull. "What's the matter with this damned Canaday anyway?" demanded a puzzled American cowboy, jailed in Battleford after a spree, *circa* 1905. "All I did was to tell the gang to throw up their hands.... Get me out o' this blamed Canaday. God's free country for mine."

No guns, no revolutions. Can any other nation in all the Americas make that statement? We did not separate violently from Europe but cut our ties cautiously in the Canadian manner — so cautiously, so imperceptibly that none of us is quite sure when we actually achieved our independence.

It is fashionable to poke fun at this Canadian caution. We have no Boston tea parties, no Valley Forges, no Bull Runs to celebrate in song and story; but then we have fewer graves to tend. In two wars fought on Canadian soil between the British and you Americans, we were minor and often unwilling participants.

We are not an impetuous people. That's a fault in some ways, for we lack the panache that goes with impetuosity, the entrepreneurial buccaneering that sometimes builds nations (and sometimes destroys them). Like the Mounted Police, we prefer to ask questions first and shoot only as a last resort. Guns make us nervous. The six-shooter has no place in our past, the handgun no place in our present.

I must say I'm always astonished when I visit your country to discover the number of people who seem to own a gun. Women keep them in their handbags, drivers in their glove compartments, businessmen in their desks. I think most of us up here were baffled when we heard that Nancy Reagan actually has a gun on her bedside table, even if it's only a little gun. Little guns fire little bullets but little bullets still kill people. And why, in the most security conscious nation and presumably, the most secure public building in the country, does the President's wife feel she must arm herself? What is she afraid of? Does she really believe that some dark night, when Ronnie is in the bathroom putting Grecian Formula on his hair, a couple of miscreants will come through the *porte cochère* to work their will upon her? It is to laugh.

In all my wide circle of friends and acquaintances here in Canada I scarcely know one who would admit to owning a handgun. Boot hills, hanging trees, necktie parties are foreign phenomena, like the Saturday night special. But then the statistics show that in your country the chances of being murdered are five times greater than in mine. And on a per capita basis we have only one quarter as many violent crimes as you.

Political assassinations are so rare — we have had only two in more than a century — that when they occur we panic and throw liberty out the window. When D'Arcy McGee, a leading political figure, was murdered on the steps of his Ottawa boardinghouse in 1868, the government suspended the Habeas Corpus Act and rounded up every Irishman it could find, fearing a Fenian uprising. In the first few days, seventy men were jailed in Toronto, Montreal and Ottawa, and held without charge or access to counsel for almost four months before being released. There is still doubt that the man who was eventually hanged for the crime was guilty.

Similar Draconian measures were invoked in October 1970, after the kidnapping of the Quebec cabinet minister, Pierre Laporte, by a cell of the separatist FLQ. On the eve of his murder habeas corpus was again suspended, our War Measures Act invoked, and 456 Quebeckers arrested in the dark of the night and held for a fortnight, again without access to counsel. Almost all were eventually released, having committed no crime.

I cannot condone any of this, Sam. I call it to your attention to underline the differences in Canadian and American attitudes. Because, you see, in each case, the majority of our people not only supported the government's authoritarian actions, they also applauded them. I remember very well the atmosphere in Toronto after the Laporte murder. "We must trust Trudeau," people were saying. Trust in big government is very much a Canadian attitude.

I don't have to make the obvious comparisons with your country, Sam, but I do find it intriguing that in spite of the frequency of assassinations in the United States, you Americans have not felt the need to act arbitrarily or throw people in jail by the score when a statesman is shot. The only defence I can make of my own people is that we abhor violence and are driven to intemperate lengths by the very whisper of revolution. It was widely believed that D'Arcy McGee was murdered by a Fenian and that an uprising of Irish fanatics was imminent; that wasn't true. It was widely believed that Pierre Laporte's death signalled what the government called "an apprehended insurrection." There isn't a smidgeon of evidence for that. Revolution is at the very root of your history; it is not part of our heritage.

Until very recently, in fact, our prime ministers have been able to walk the streets of Ottawa, tipping their hats to passers-by, without any worries except, perhaps, for the occasional catcall. The cloud of security men who surround your president on his rare trips to our country astonishes and even amuses us.

I will always remember Lester Pearson sauntering into an Ottawa TV studio for a half-hour interview with me, accompanied only by his press secretary, and inquiring casually of the receptionist where the make-up room was located. In my mind's eye, I saw your president arriving by motorcade, secret service men clustering around him like hornets, entire carloads of reporters trailing behind, a huge throng of onlookers held back by police cordons. But here, even the station manager remained in his office and the receptionist scarcely looked up. I suppose we should be appalled by this lack of ostentation; I suspect, however, that most Canadians would find it rather endearing.

*N*ow, Sam, I want you to come back with me to my old home town in the summer of 1898 to meet a nubile young woman named Freda Maloof, who calls herself the Turkish Whirlwind Danseuse, although, to be accurate, she is Greek.

Here she comes, moving sinuously across the stage of Joe Cooper's false-fronted Tivoli Theatre, the muscles of her remarkable tummy moving in cadence to the music of the band. Her appearance, alas, is brief. The hootchie-kootchie dance, which did more for Chicago's Columbian Exposition than Louis Sullivan's architecture, has been judged too immoral for Dawson

City. At Wrangell, on the Alaska Panhandle, this same stampede summer, the famous German hurdy-gurdy girls are displaying unspeakable amounts of naked flesh; but in Canada's woolliest community, decorum must be observed.

The villain of the piece is actually an authentic Canadian hero, with a barrel chest and a fierce pair of waxed mustaches, Superintendent Sam Steele, assigned to bring order out of chaos in Dawson City even if it means limiting our right to watch a belly dance.

This incident should not surprise any Canadian, because the Mounted Police have a long tradition of bending the law when it suits their purpose — that purpose always being the protection of the public, not only against violence and accident, but also against sedition, treason, immorality and similar horrors. In this, the police are only the instruments of the government and the government is clearly responding to the will of the voters. For if the majority of Canadians *wanted* the police to stop bending the law, then the police would stop.

Oh, we had our typical Canadian crimes. Chopping your own wood on a Sunday was one. We Canadians take the Lord's Day seriously. Just this year a Toronto book store was hauled into court and fined for daring to disturb the Sabbath peace by actually selling books. In Dawson, the Lord's Day was as peaceful — and as dull — as it was in the rest of Canada. Even dog races were banned. Two men were actually fined for examining their fish nets on Sunday; that's how tight the law was.

The Canadian authorities not only protected the town's morals, as Miss Maloof discovered, they also protected the Queen's reputation. Steele acted as a political censor, banning from the stage of Dawson's many theatres any remarks that he considered disrespectful of sovereign, country or empire. He did so for what he considered the best of reasons, just as those of his successors who burned a barn in Quebec and committed other breaches of the law believed that they, too, were doing no more than their duty — protecting us from treasonous separatists and God knows what else.

Again, I'm not necessarily condoning these attitudes. But I'm trying to emphasize that, historically, Canadians put order first, individual freedom second. I think it's fair to say that for most of our history we have tended to look askance at what we considered to be a permissive society below the border. "Liberty," in our northern view, is alarmingly close to "libertine."

Steele's theatrical censorship was part of a Canadian tradition that continues to this day. Forty years after he expunged a satirical remark about Her Majesty from the Dawson stage, Canada banned the American magazine *Ken* because it carried on its cover a caricature of King George VI and his queen. *Life* received the same treatment for daring to run photos of a baby's birth. A Robert Sherwood play at Toronto's Royal Alexandra theatre was censored as lewd in the mid-thirties because of an overly long stage kiss. In postwar Ontario there were continual controversies over nude paintings gracing the walls of the Canadian National Exhibition's art gallery.

I remember opening a rather tame exhibit of so-called erotic art at an established Toronto gallery in the 1960s and remarking that the town had finally grown up. I could not have been more wrong. The following day the police arrived, closed the show and haled the gallery's owner, Dorothy Cameron, into court where she was fined for presenting an obscene exhibit.

To this day there are no X-rated movies in Canada as there are in most major American cities. With certain exceptions, we now allow your skin magazines on our newsstands, but only after some discreet editorial cover-up. Placed strategically over certain crotch shots, the maple leaf has become a fig leaf, a curious use for a national symbol, wouldn't you say?

I'm talking about the whole country, Sam — about Nova Scotians and Albertans, Ontarians and Quebeckers. In these areas, the province of Quebec is not separatist. Everything I've been telling you about — the respect for authority, the hunger for security, the yearning for peace, order and good, strong government, the rejection of the permissive and the "libertine" — are national qualities that unite us all.

In this sense, Maurice Duplessis's Padlock Law and René Lévesque's Language Bill are of a piece. Both premiers were trying to protect their people by means that you might feel Draconian: Duplessis protecting them from the Communists by padlocking the doors of the suspected Reds in the thirties; Lévesque protecting them from the English tongue in the Sixties by banning all non-French signs. In both cases Quebec got a strong government and order over liberty. The two laws fit the Canadian style. Like their English-speaking cousins, Quebeckers have always followed the national instinct to put security ahead of civil rights.

It's no accident that French Canadian Roman Catholics have historically been part of the ultramontane wing of the church — the Puritan wing. This is a Puritan country. Blue laws may vary from region to region and from decade to decade but Quebec, in common with every other province, has a motion picture censor board. And certain books deemed wicked or subversive are stopped at the Quebec border, as at other provincial borders, by federal immigration officials who do not need to give any reason for their actions or even reveal the titles on the banned list. It's true that beer is sold in grocery stores in Montreal, but I would bet it's the only city of its size on the continent that does not have a massage parlour.

I don't think I need to labour the point. If our protective authority cushions us from want, unemployment and sudden medical catastrophe, it also saves us from our so-called instincts. And that is the way we have wanted it since those far-off days when, in resisting American military incursion, we also found ourselves resisting some aspects of what we like to call, with a mixture of envy and censure, "the American way of life."

THREE

Once a Loyalist...

Historically, a Canadian is an American who rejects the revolution.

NORTHROP FRYE, 1953

*D*ear Sam:

You're right to wonder how it all came about. As you say, the Mountie is only the symbol of something deep within the Canadian psyche and my Yukon examples only expressions of an attitude that must go a long way back. I could have given you similar examples from the Fraser River and Cariboo gold rushes of British Columbia which took place long before the Mounties were invented. Here you find the same startling contrast between your frontier and ours. Even some of the same anecdotes are told about Sam Steele and his British Columbia counterpart, Judge Matthew Baillie Begbie, the man who brought peace, order and tough government to the interior of British Columbia.

"We won't put up with your bullying here,"

Begbie-Steele is supposed to have told an American bad man. "The fine is one hundred dollars."

"That's all right," comes the jaunty reply. "I've got that in my pocket."

"And six months' hard labour. Have you got that in your pocket, too?"

So let's go a long way back — 80 years before Begbie's Cariboo, 116 years before Steele's Klondike, and meet an ancestor of mine, my great-great-great-grandfather, Captain Peter Berton. In 1784, Captain Berton, a well-to-do Oyster Bay merchant and shipmaster, packed it up, quit Long Island and brought a shipload of his fellow Americans to what he described in the family Bible as "the whiles of Noviscotia."

You would call Peter Berton a Tory, which he certainly was, for he refused the pleas of his radical friends to fight against the British. He preferred instead, in those chaotic revolutionary days, to take his chances on the shores of what he wryly admitted was "a cold and barren uncomfortable countrey." We Canadians, however, do not call him a Tory; to us, he is a Loyalist. "Loyal" has been a much-used word in our past, as "liberty" has been in yours.

I call my ancestor to mind, Sam, because you have asked me how it can be that two peoples who appear so much alike and who share the same continent can be so dissimilar. The border is invisible; why are we not the same? I think there are several reasons: geography, ethnic background — even climate. But history has as much to do with it as these and my ancestor and his fellow Loyalists, suffering through those first terrible winters at Oak Point on the Saint John River, are part of that history.

Our history can be said to lack passion. That may be one reason why we do not wear our emotions on our sleeves as you do. Our ancestors did not engage in civil disobedience at Boston or take up arms against British redcoats. This does not mean that our forebears were entirely content under British rule but they lacked the opportunity and, let's face it, the passionate desire to rebel. Our Atlantic colonies depended on Great Britain to a far greater extent than your famous Thirteen. Newfoundland had no experience with democracy, Nova Scotia very little. British sea power made American conquest impossible and your raids along our coast got the people's backs up so that even the newly arrived Americans declined to revolt.

The merchants of Montreal and Quebec were little more than an economic colony of Great Britain, largely dependent on London for their existence. And again, the American attack on Montreal and the siege of Quebec united the mass of the people against invaders who seemed to be more like conquerors than liberators. In contrast to those who followed Wolfe, your leaders clearly despised the French Canadians and their church.

Meanwhile, in my ancestor's words, "thousands of poor, distressed families has been tumbled into this poor, impoverished countrey." Fifty thousand refugees poured into Canada, helping to form a new province — New Brunswick — which was 90 per cent Loyalist.

Thousands also crossed the border into the wilderness that is now southern Ontario. Most of these were people who had refused to take the law into their own hands, who opted neither for liberty nor death and who, for a variety of reasons — not always unselfish — preferred the status quo.

Having endured the enmity and often the brutality of their fellows to move to a strange and often forbidding land, these newcomers were scarcely in a mood to embrace the new American political ideas. Anyone who studies the documents of those post-revolutionary days will realize what wicked words "democracy" and "republicanism" were to the Canadian elite, which swiftly included Loyalists as well as British-born. Those words stood for evil, in the same way that "communism" stands for evil in the minds of many people today.

The Loyalists in Canada have had an influence out of all proportion to their numbers. They were, after all, the Chosen and they soon occupied positions of leadership and power. It will astonish you, I'm sure, when I tell you that thousands of their descendants proudly call themselves Loyalists to this day and even hold Loyalist conventions. Once a Loyalist, always a Loyalist.

My father was one of these: loyal to the Church of England, which he saw as a bulwark against radical and un-British nonconformism; loyal to the British connection — like the others, he called himself a United *Empire* Loyalist; and loyal to the Conservative party, which we Canadians still dub the Tory party.

My earliest memories are tied up with that same family Bible in which Peter Berton described his arrival on those cold and barren Atlantic shores. My father used to read those passages aloud to us, showing us the cramped, brown handwriting, then 150 years old. Thus, in far-off Dawson City, we felt the tug of our heritage. I still have that Bible and I cannot turn those brittle pages without feeling a little tingle, as if a ghost had just brushed past.

We think of Ontario as a true-blue province, Sam, and with good reason. In its early days, when it was called Upper Canada, it was populated almost entirely by Loyalists and by the families of British soldiers who had fought against your ancestors. At the time of your Revolution, it was an empty wilderness. When the Americans began to pour in, every effort was made to convince them that loyalty was more rewarding than rebellion; and so it must have seemed to many of them. For the land was free and the taxes were low. The British government footed the bill for almost everything: pensions, soldiers' pay, Indian presents, the salaries of public servants.

Pretty soon more Americans got the idea that Upper Canada was, if not the Promised Land, certainly a land of promise. This caused a certain amount of confusion. The bulk of the ruling elite was convinced that these people were fleeing across the border because they couldn't stand the wicked American political system — "the spirit of levelling," as it was snobbishly called. Not true, Sam. Your former countrymen were not so much interested in political philosophies as they were in getting ahead.

By 1812, the powers-that-be had awoken to the fact that Upper Canada was predominantly American. The newcomers now outnumbered the Loyalists and the British, who continued to monopolize power and who had no intention of relinquishing it. Still, the settlers were proving unsettling. Francis Gore, the governor, was one of those who worried about "new settlers . . . of doubtful loyalty," who retained subversive ideas "of equality and insubordination."

Now here is the supreme irony. If things had continued in this way, I think it possible, even probable, that Upper Canada would have become an American state simply through the osmosis of continued immigration. It didn't because you Americans declared war on Great Britain and tried, unsuccessfully, to take the upper province by force.

At first, all you wanted to do was teach the British a lesson for arrogance on the high seas during the Napoleonic blockade. But later, there was talk of outright annexation. And again there was confusion about national attitudes. The American leadership was convinced that their former countrymen would rise up and throw off the British yoke once an American army crossed the border. In this they were as myopic as the Upper Canadian leadership, which thought the new arrivals had come to Canada to throw off the American yoke.

Actually these new Upper Canadians just wanted

to be left alone to till the rich, cheap land and make a good living. It's true that they had little say in their own political destinies but that did not bother them unduly. The British yoke was so light that most did not feel it. Many sympathized with their former compatriots; some, in fact, tried to help the invaders, especially during the attack on York, now Toronto. But they did not rise up and flock to Old Glory when General Hull's troops made their brief foray across the Detroit River or when General Dearborn's riflemen landed in Toronto Bay. Whether they liked it or not — and a good many did *not* — the war helped turn them into Canadians. And much of the credit for that (or, you might say, blame) must go to another immigrant, a Scot of powerful personality named John Strachan.

*O*nly a handful of my countrymen, Sam, have heard of John Strachan, although almost everyone in Toronto the Good knows of Bishop Strachan School, which is a private institution for the daughters of the privileged. When I encounter one of these Bishop Strachan ladies I cannot help feeling a little grubby, and a bit awkward, too, for these are cool and elegant young women, coolly and expensively coiffured, their dress also cool, expensive, understated. A boy from the Yukon can be permitted to feel slightly gauche in their presence. The word "Bishop Strachan" connotes Upper Class; and that fits, for John Strachan, long before he became bishop of Toronto, believed in a class system — the very antithesis of American democracy — in which a privileged and educated elite would guide the destinies of the nation.

Here he comes, moving briskly along the muddy cobblestones of York, on the eve of the American attack, which will entrench him as the unofficial power in Upper Canada — the chaplain of York, a swarthy Scot, dourly handsome, a man of strong opinions and phlegmatic mien.

What are these strong opinions? Mainly, they are pro-British and anti-American. Strachan believes, for instance, that George III, the villain of your history books, is perhaps the most perfect human being on earth, "the faithful guardian and dispenser of all benefits." Generous, benevolent, just, the mad old king's greatest joy, in Strachan's belief, "is to see his subjects happy and free." His is "the most perfect form of government," and "we are the subjects of his paternal care."

Oh, I can see you bristling over all that. If Strachan became the most influential man of his time, holding those views, we begin to understand how Canada was set on a different course from the United States. Strachan, in common with the British and the Loyalist leadership, had little use for Americans or the American system. "Liberty" to him was "licentious liberty." The Americans, in his eyes, were vulgar, common people and so were the American immigrants.

"To give you an idea of the common people here,"

he wrote to a friend and mentor in the old country, "it is necessary to remind you that almost all are Americans." There was, he believed, "a lamentable want of independent, respectable people...plenty of them have acquired property but in point of information, they are brutes."

American republicanism, in Strachan's view, was irreligious and materialistic. Americans were money-grubbers: "*vain and rapacious* and without *honor* — they are hurried to any action provided they gain money by it." As for American democracy, it was closer to anarchy: "The frequency of their elections keeps them in a continual broil to promote the interests of their factions." I have to confess that vestiges of this attitude linger on to this day.

Strachan believed firmly in an established Church of England as the dominant force to shore up the loyalty of Canadians against the pernicious influence of the Methodist circuit-riders who were pouring into Upper Canada and "filling the country with most deplorable fanaticism." The Methodists, in Strachan's eyes, symbolized the loud, vulgar ebullience of American democracy: "They will bawl, twenty of them at once, tumble on the ground, laugh, sing, jump and stamp, and this they call the working of the Spirit."

As for the tenuous democracy practised in his own province, Strachan despised it. The weak lower house of the legislature — the only elected body — was, in his opinion, composed of "ignorant clowns." The real decisions were made by the British governor and his appointed council, a council in which Strachan and his coterie were soon to play a leading role.

For the War of 1812 turned Strachan into a civilian hero. During the attack on York, this implacable cleric stood up to the American high command and bullied it into making concessions. Faced with the imperturbable chaplain challenging him in his thick Scots brogue, Dearborn, the commander, might well have asked himself who was the conquerer and who the conquered.

And so it was John Strachan and his followers who set the political style in the postwar years. His own protégés — sons of the privileged who attended his famous school at Cornwall — climbed quickly into positions of power for, being Loyalist or British, they were not tainted with American ideas. Strachan had seen to that. You've got to hand it to him, Sam. None of what I've told you was an accident; from the very beginning, this remarkable clergyman had intended that his students should aspire to and achieve leadership. He himself became the acknowledged head of the elite group, many of them intermarried, who came to be called the Family Compact.

I know you haven't heard of the Family Compact but most Canadian schoolboys know something about it — enough to know that these people, appointed not elected, dominated the affairs of Upper Canada for the best part of the nineteenth century. Their influence can still be felt, not only in Ontario but also in the rest of Canada. It waned over the years, of course, as the radicals grew in power and demands for a more responsible form of government grew more insistent. We even had a small, unsatisfactory rebellion in Upper Canada and another in Lower Canada at the same time, both suppressed without much difficulty and with a minimum of spilled blood.

We achieved our form of democracy gradually, almost imperceptibly in our cautious Canadian way. "Experience and observation," wrote Strachan, "teach me to modify my improvements and to adapt them with caution." Did you know, Sam, that we save twice as much of our disposable income as you do? We are not a nation of big spenders; we prefer to be safe, not sorry.

The War of 1812 made it easy to ward off American ideas and influences because you Americans had become The Enemy. Who would dare advocate enemy political philosophies after the attack on York and the burning of Newark? During the war, certain York farmers were thrown into jail for statements overheard in taverns praising American democracy; in the postwar years it was a bold man who would repeat those statements. Most were content to accept, at least in public, a different political system.

Not only that, but John Strachan and his associates used the war as a kind of rallying point to unite everybody who lived north of the border. Mythology is important to any nation, as you Americans have long realized. Strachan helped to unite Upper Canada's indifferent farmers by telling them repeatedly that *they* had won the war. He believed it and eventually just about everyone in the new province of Ontario came to believe it, including the sons and daughters of ex-Americans. It did not matter that Strachan's view of the war was just that — a myth; that most of the battles were won by British regulars and Indians. For all of the nineteenth and much of the twentieth century, Strachan's view prevailed. *We* had hurled the Americans back. *We* had won the war. *We* would have, in a later political phrase, "no truck nor trade with the Yankees."

The Family Compact believed firmly that the American system was open to corruption because of the short terms of the elected officials, and that it was also contrary to the laws of nature and of God. True government was derived not from the governed at the grass roots but from the King on high, from religion through an established church, and from the conventions and experiences of the past. These ideas have lingered. It has not been easy to exorcise John Strachan's ghost. His shade was there at Miles Canyon when Steele of the Mounted laid down the law from on high. And it continues to haunt us to this very day.

I have a theory, Sam, about how the War of 1812 helped distort our view of your countrymen. For in that foolish conflict, Canadians for the first time encountered a different kind of American. These were not the easy-going farmers who lived as neighbours just across the Detroit and Niagara rivers or just south of the

Eastern Townships of Quebec. These were Southerners — Indian fighters, backwoodsmen, brawlers and eye-gougers — individuals all. The war was fought largely by this kind of soldier, Kentuckians mainly. Sixty-four per cent of all the American casualties in the War of 1812 were suffered by young men from that state.

Thus, in the years that followed, when Canadians heard the word "British," they could not help seeing a line of disciplined men, uniformed, marching in perfect order. But the word "American" conjured up a different vision: a horde of ragged frontiersmen, slipping like phantoms through the trees, squirrel rifles at the alert, each acting on his own — a mob of wild men, perfectly prepared to take a scalp or burn a house in defiance of orders. In Montreal, curious crowds came down to stare at the Kentucky prisoners captured at French-town, as if they were visitors from another planet. Surprisingly, they seemed almost human.

As in the Revolution, your soldiers did not always play by the accepted rules of warfare, which said that each man must stand shoulder to shoulder with his fellows and advance without ducking or flinching in the face of enemy fire, each man a small, disciplined cog in a well-oiled military juggernaut. This worked well on the field but not in the woods. "Show us our enemy," the redcoats cried plaintively at York, as the Americans peppered them from behind tree trunks and boulders.

Your militia even *elected* their officers and did so until the eve of the Great War, a piece of egalitarianism that baffled the Canadians and, to be fair, also irked the

American regulars. As a young subaltern in World War
Two and as a war correspondent in Korea, I saw
something of your troops and was mystified, as were
my fellow Canadians, by the camaraderie that existed
between officers and men. Why, some even called their
superiors by their first names!

If the British-Canadian victories at Queenston
Heights and Crysler's Farm are now part of our school-
book mythology, it is, I think, precisely because in
these encounters order and discipline saved the day for
our side. Here, on flat ground, the thin red line drove
the Americans over the cliffs of the Niagara gorge and
sent them scurrying back to the gunboats at Cook's
Point. Thus, in the postwar years, the sight of the Union
Jack fluttering over the Governor's mansion must have
seemed strangely comforting to those Canadians who,
when they thought of freedom at all, thought in terms
of freedom from the Americans.

Oddly, since most of the fighting was done by
southerners and westerners, the contempt that the
Canadian elite held for their former enemies was
distilled into the single epithet "Yankee." Even today
that word can have unpleasant connotations. When we
call somebody a Yankee we are not about to praise
him. It was the favourite pejorative of our first prime
minister, John A. Macdonald, who kept insisting
that he was born and would die a British subject;
by which he meant *not* American. When William
Van Horne first arrived from Michigan to build the
CPR, Macdonald called him a "sharp Yankee" —

the ultimate malediction. Later, I'm sure, he came to regret that.

John Strachan held the same view. And, as anyone who studies the political journals of the nineteenth century will discover, it persisted well into the twentieth. The Yankees were "sharp"; their God was Mammon. They were also vulgar, uncouth, and they talked funny. In the pages of *Grip*, the famous political weekly, and *The Moon*, the satirical journal, Uncle Sam and his predecessor Brother Jonathan invariably speak in a kind of comic stage dialect, saying things like "Wa'al, I calc'late" or "Tarnation, I reckon…."

My maternal grandfather contributed to many of those journals. I can still see him in his mid-eighties, white-bearded and rheumy-eyed, sitting at his roll-top desk in Oakville, dictating to his youngest daughter, my Aunt Maude, while I, a boy of eleven, visiting from the far-off Yukon, lay stomach down on the living-room rug, poring through copies of *The Moon*, which was full of funny and often wicked cartoons and caricatures.

Let us go back to *The Moon* of 1902 and 1903 and leaf through these volumes to see what they tell us about Canadian attitudes to your countrymen.

Here is Uncle Sam, lean as Cassius, explaining to a plump and protesting John Bull why he broke his promise and did not select "three eminent jurists" to sit on the Alaska Boundary Commission: "They ain't Jurists ef you mean Jedges, but they're three smart cusses and I calc'late they'll do the Jewin' for me all right!"

Here is the famous *Moon* series lampooning The

American Girl, a perennial subject in your own magazines of that day. No. 1 shows a toothy young woman with a vast coiffure, sparkling with overweight jewelry, pulling a wad of gum from her mouth:

> *Sweet Sylvia with the winking eye*
> *And teeth just built for biting pie*
> *And chewing gum.*

And here is Uncle Sam, looking more villainous than ever, down on his knees, holding a sack of bullion over his head, worshipping "Strange Gods." On pedestals before him are the objects of his adulation: *Sensation Drama*; *Yellow Journal*; *Celebrated Actress*; *Humbug*; *Coon Songs*; *Foreign Nobleman*; *Wealthy Parvenue*; *Burlesque*.

All manifestly unfair, Sam, and more than a little racist. I am not at all sure that the mass of the Canadian public held these views. But the point is that the people to whom these journals catered — the literate elite, the pro-British, pro-Loyalist upper classes, certainly did. It was, to be fair, their form of protection against foreign influences, which they felt to be dangerous to the country. The only way to fight American values was to make them appear vulgar and vaguely comic.

This attitude persists. Some of my countrymen sneer at American television as vulgar and commercial while watching it avidly. In my youth, Hollywood movies got the same treatment. To my chagrin, after we left the north my mother insisted on taking me to the

Empire theatre in Victoria, which showed only British films, because she believed they were more uplifting than the products from south of the border. She refused to admit that most of the British films of that day were rubbish.

Compared to you, we are not good salesmen and we are not good showmen. And it is my theory that one of the reasons for this springs out of the attitude I've been describing. It goes like this, Sam: Americans are good at blowing their own horn, but Americans are vulgar; therefore blowing your own horn is vulgar. Thus advertising is vulgar, the hard sell is "sharp," showbusiness is crass. To a large degree we have shunned commercialism in our culture, much of which is publicly subsidized. Yours isn't. Yet without these public subsidies we are in danger of being swamped by you.

Thus our identity has also been shaped by our negative reaction to your overpowering presence. We know who we are *not* even if we aren't quite sure who we are. We are not American. But are we masculine or feminine? The political cartoonists of the last century were never certain. When resisting American encroachment, Canada was depicted as a virile young pioneer in a Stetson kicking Uncle Sam or Brother Jonathan in the pants. When fending off American blandishments, Canada was shown as a long-tressed virgin, resisting the advances of an amorous Uncle Sam. And these seductive advances and threatened encroachments are still at the heart of Canadian public policy.

*P*erhaps you don't remember the phrase, "manifest destiny," Sam; it's gone out of style in your country. But many Canadians remember it well, for it once fell trippingly from the tongues of American politicians and journalists who believed it was America's manifest destiny to stretch its boundaries northward to the Arctic, or at least to that parallel of latitude that produced the jingoist phrase "Fifty-four forty or fight!" It was manifest destiny that forced the confederation of the British provinces north of that border in 1867. And it was manifest destiny, as expressed by the Minnesota expansionists in the same period, that forced the construction of the Canadian Pacific Railway.

Long before that we were reacting, as we have always reacted to the American initiative, by government-sponsored mega-projects. The Rideau Canal, built between Kingston and Ottawa, was the first. It is a beautiful and placid waterway, not much wider than a modern pleasure craft, bordered by summer cottages and green lawns. It gives Ottawa much of its charm, for it cuts directly through the capital, rising eighty feet from the river through a staircase of eight ancient locks in the shadow of the Chateau Laurier.

Whenever I look down on those locks from my hotel window I think back with astonishment at the incredible feat of engineering and the back-breaking labour that produced it. Think of it: 123 miles of canal, all of it dug by hand, with shovel and wheelbarrow in the days before steam shovels and bulldozers; 47 locks, all hand-fashioned from local stone, and the entire project completed in just six years, from 1826 to 1832!

But why? A water link already existed between the two Canadas — the St. Lawrence River. Why another? The answer, of course, is that the Canadians of those days feared another American invasion and desperately wanted a second lifeline between the provinces. The canal was built not for private profit but as a public project; and that is the way things have been in my country ever since.

From the days of the Rideau Canal to the year of Petro-Canada, we have been a public-enterprise country. As one of our more perceptive analysts, Herschel Hardin, has pointed out, public enterprise is indigenous to the Canadian form of democracy. Leaving the financial institutions aside, one-third of all Canadian-controlled corporate assets are held by those distinctively Canadian institutions, the crown corporations; and our greatest entrepreneurs — such men as John A. Macdonald, C.D. Howe, W.A.C. Bennett, Adam Beck and René Lévesque, to name a handful — have been politicians, not businessmen.

A few months ago I was invited to Chicago to speak to a convention of American oil men who were convinced, I think, that our government was socialist and our prime minister a Red. These business people could not fathom our National Energy Policy in any other context. They looked baffled when I told them that most Canadian socialists consider Mr. Trudeau an economic right winger and that, if the polls are to be believed, most Canadians are strongly in favour of a National Energy Policy, while the sales figures indicate that our publicly owned oil company is a howling success.

I also tried to explain what I am explaining to you: that our various experiments in public owner- ship have nothing to do with political dogma but are, instead, a reaction to American initiatives. Ontario Hydro, one of the earliest and most successful of our publicly owned utilities, was launched by Adam Beck, who was about as far from being a socialist as David Rockefeller. He was, in fact, a rock-ribbed Ontario Tory, a minister in the Conservative govern- ment of the day, who believed and said publicly that no Canadian would ever tolerate the political sub- serviency that would result if the Americans cornered our energy market. As a result, he is an authentic Canadian hero, immortalized by an imposing statue on Toronto's University Avenue.

When our economic or our cultural sovereignty is threatened, profit has always taken a back seat to the national interest. William Hamilton Merritt, who promoted our largest canal, the Welland, was a pri- vate enterpriser; yet he insisted that canals were not for private gain. Like the railways and airlines that followed, like the utilities and broadcasting net- works, the research council, film board, national bank, ferry systems and a host of other publicly owned corporations ranging all the way from a seed company to a steel mill, they form the bricks and mortar in the national bulwark we were forced to construct to protect ourselves from you.

You must also remember that our domestic market is one-tenth the size of yours. In instance after instance when private enterprise has faltered, the government has had to move in, as it did in the early twenties when two national railroads went to the wall — and as it is preparing to do, even as I write this, with Dome Petroleum. Nobody in this country calls this socialism, especially when the device of the crown corporation helps keep politics at arms length from these publicly owned businesses. In fact, in a surprising number of cases, the impetus for these takeovers has come from right-wing, conservative governments.

Sam, let us go back to July of 1952 and look in on a little scene in a suite in the Empress Hotel, that vine-covered chateau on Government Street, Victoria. The suite belongs to A.E. "Dal" Grauer, the darkly handsome president of the B.C. Electric Company, the province's largest privately owned utility. Grauer is in the middle of a forceful discussion with two of British Columbia's most influential journalists: Bruce Hutchison, Canada's most respected and eloquent newspaperman, editor of the Victoria *Times*, and his publisher, Stuart Keate. Like Grauer, both are staunch Liberals, federally and provincially, but now the provincial Liberal party is in disarray, reduced to a corporal's guard in the legislature, swamped by a new, untried party calling itself Social Credit.

Because of the new transferable vote in the province, the political situation is still fluid. The socialist CCF has garnered almost as many seats as Social Credit. It is clear that the new movement will form a minority government under the ebullient leadership of a one-time hardware merchant and ex-Conservative named W.A.C. Bennett. It is also clear that the two old parties are in real trouble in British Columbia and that the political spectrum will be dominated by the socialists on the left and the Social Credit, despite its confusing name, on the right.

Grauer has come to Victoria to enlist the support of the two journalists for what he rightly calls "the free enterprise party." I stay in the background, a guest of Hutchison's, and listen to the B.C. Electric's key man declare that all those who oppose socialism must stand together to back this strange new force in the province and its untested leader. Otherwise — well, I don't think he actually said it — but what Dal Grauer feared most in those confused days, when nobody really knew who had won the election, was a CCF victory. For a CCF victory would mean the certain takeover of Grauer's company.

Now comes the bitter irony; you won't believe it. Nobody has ever called Wacky Bennett a socialist. In fact, he won election after election denouncing what he called "the Socialist hordes." When he nationalized the B.C. ferry system, nobody called it socialism. When he extended the government-owned railway into the north, nobody called it socialism. And when he rose in the legislature on August 1, 1961 and, in the shortest speech of his career — a mere fifty seconds — announced the government's takeover of the B.C. Electric, nobody called that socialism, either.

Certainly not Dal Grauer, who, at that very moment — three in the afternoon, just after the stock market closed — was being borne to his rest through the streets of Vancouver, cut off in the prime of life by leukemia. As Bennett, following a long Canadian tradition, turned the B.C. Electric into a crown corporation, the funeral cortège passed by the glittering building which was once a Grauer fief and now, at the stroke of a pen, belonged to the people.

FOUR

Of kilts
and babushkas

---

*You will be better Canadians
for being Ukrainians....*

LORD TWEEDSMUIR, 1936

---

*D*ear Sam:

Today is my birthday but that's not why I'm writing. It's also Orangemen's Day, though the Orangemen will not be parading on a busy Monday. They've lost their clout in Canada and so must take a back seat to traffic and march down the streets of small towns on weekends. Even here in Toronto, the stronghold of the Order, the parade that once brought business to a halt, with thousands crammed along the streets hoping for a glimpse of King Billy on his white horse, is but a shadow of its former self. And besides, the Italians have taken over the town, having won the World Soccer Cup. There are far more Italian flags to be seen on the streets today than there were Canadian flags showing on July 1.

The Irish Protestants are part of our traditional ethnic mix, the subject of this letter; the Italians, as yet, are not. But before I get to the Irish and all the other ancestral groups that have helped to make us the kind of people we are, I want to respond to your point that Americans and Canadians both spring from Anglo-Celtic stock. That's not exactly true: our rulers have certainly been Anglo-Celtic; but here in Canada, the ruled have come from a variety of backgrounds.

This ethnic stew is not the same as yours. You must be aware of two obvious differences when you visit my country: the French presence and the black absence. The French language hits you as soon as you arrive at one of our airports. When I visit one of your cities, the first thing I notice is the number of black faces in the crowd.

The blacks are scarcely noticeable in Canada. One of the several reasons why our history lacks violence is that, by and large, we have no urban constituency of the dispossessed — no black ghettoes bubbling and seething beneath the placid metropolitan overburden. The reasons for this reflect no credit on us any more than the reasons for the black presence in America reflect any credit on your forebears.

We kept the blacks out and we did it in a peculiarly Canadian fashion — by pretending publicly that our immigration laws did not discriminate against anyone by reason of race, creed or colour while at the same time preventing all Negroes from crossing the border into Canada. We achieved that by enforcing border inspections to the point of absurdity during the great immigration boom before World War One. At White Rock, British Columbia, to take only one instance, a group of forty blacks attempted to enter the country. All were turned back because the medical inspection officer swore that every last one was suffering from tuberculosis.

This was standard procedure. The Commissioner for Immigration for Western Canada actually paid a fee to the medical inspector at Emerson, Manitoba, for every black he rejected. In fact, black leaders in the United States were quietly told by our government that border inspections would invariably mean rejection. That policy, of course, was never publicly enunciated. Instead, immigration officials fell back on the old argument that Negroes couldn't stand the fierce Canadian climate. Ironically, that statement was issued in the very same year in which a black explorer was one of the first two men to reach the North Pole.

The real reason for the rejection of blacks was enunciated by the Toronto *Mail and Empire* in April 1911 when, in demanding a total ban on black immigration, it declared that "Canada wants no Negro question ... no race riots."

Our largest cities — Toronto and Montreal — have a black minority, mostly from the Caribbean but we have no rioting blacks in Canada, though we have had rioting whites opposing Orientals in British Columbia. It is, I think, our loss. For there is no doubt that your own culture has been immeasurably enriched by the black presence.

So we have no black problem and you have no French problem. We have peaceable cities but unpeaceable provinces. The regional tensions that exist in my country are partly the result of geography, as I shall argue a little later, but they also spring from the French presence. What Quebec is given, in the interests of preserving national unity, the other provinces demand. Latterly, this attempt to satisfy all has disturbed the regional balance in my country. There are some who insist that these intense regional rivalries — French versus English, West versus East, provinces versus Ottawa, Canadians versus Americans — are at the root of our national identity. After all, that's what being a Canadian is all about; it gives us kinetic energy, distinguishing us from other countries. I think there is a good deal of truth in that. But, my God, Sam, it's been an exhausting business. Because it's also true that our preoccupation with these regional problems has drained us emotionally, using up precious energy that might be diverted to other forms of nation-building. Just as the black problem has obsessed you, diverting you from more positive pursuits, so our problem with Quebec and the regions has preoccupied us to the point of stagnation.

"Separatism" is a very Canadian word, as old as Confederation. Nova Scotia had scarcely joined the new federal state when a huge chunk of the population demanded it get right out again. In Victoria, in 1876, a secret society, "The Carnarvon Club," sprang up advocating out and out separation from mainland

British Columbia; one of its members was the premier's son. In my day, the letters page of the Victoria *Colonist* was crammed with angry epistles demanding that Vancouver Island be returned to the status of a crown colony.

There are other distinctively Canadian words and phrases which are foreign to your lexicon. "National unity" is one; I doubt that you or any of your friends toss that subject around at the dinner table, but we do. "Ethnicity" is another, along with "multiculturalism." We have an entire government department devoted to that, if you can believe it. It's a relatively new cabinet post but the rationale goes back to the Conquest — a word that has been expunged from our dictionary of Canadianisms.

For when the British allowed the French to retain their customs, culture, language and religion, they set the future nation of Canada on a special course. It was inevitable that what the French received as a legal right, other language groups would soon demand. We don't talk about a melting pot here in Canada — never have. We boast, instead, about our "Canadian mosaic," another distinctive phrase that will be new to you. Actually, it's relatively new to us, too. I've been reading the western Canadian newspapers for those immigrant years after the turn of the century and it's quite clear that the Eastern Europeans' success or failure was measured not only in terms of economic prosperity but also in the speed with which they learned English and adopted Canadian customs. The *Manitoba Free Press*, praising the Ukrainians in 1902, noted that "they adapt themselves with much rapidity to Canadian manners" and wrote approvingly of one girl who "would not admit she was Galician but claimed to be Scotch...."

Yet in spite of this, the *idea* of the melting pot never caught on. Our ethnic minorities have managed to retain their identity and are now being praised for having done so. How did this happen? Perhaps because we did not ask them to make the kind of commitment to their new homeland that you did. How could we? One-third of our people thought of Canada almost entirely in terms of a single region, French-speaking. The other two-thirds were committed to England. The frontispiece in my school reader said it all — a picture of the Union Jack (we had no flag of our own) and the slogan: "One Flag, One Fleet, One Throne." The commitment was not to country but to Empire — to Europe. Who could blame the immigrants for following our lead?

There was no ringing rhetoric in Canada about self-evident truths, about all men being created equal, or about the poor, tired, huddled masses. That's revolutionary idealism. It's quite clear from the newspapers of the day that Canadians didn't care to have poor, huddled masses moving in next door. "We do not want here the scum of Europe," cried Montreal's *La Patrie* and this sentiment was echoed by the Calgary *Herald*, the Edmonton *Bulletin* and the Winnipeg *Tribune*. What we really wanted were well-to-do, right-thinking English farmers. Unfortunately these had no intention of leaving so we settled for those Europeans who came to Canada to escape intolerable conditions at home; and we lured them, in our stolid Canadian way, not with romantic slogans but with the promise of free homesteads and rich farmland. Canada was advertised not as the land of the brave and the home of the free but as a place to make money.

Thus, the much-touted mosaic is the result of good old Canadian compromise, an adjustment to the kind of tensions produced when reality doesn't match up with the ideal. We wanted proper-thinking Brits; we got Slavic peasants. So we made a virtue out of ethnicity; and ever since we've gone along with those groups who want to retain something of their original culture, language and dress — like the Quebeckers. It's said, for instance, that more Gaelic is spoken on Cape Breton Island than in all of Scotland. The onion-shaped domes of the Greek and Ukrainian Orthodox churches are as familiar to our prairie landscape as the grain elevator. In Canada, where Italian flags can outnumber maple leafs and half the short-wave radios in the Dufferin area of Toronto are tuned to Rome, the babushka is almost as familiar as the kilt.

If a man wore a kilt on the streets of one of your cities, Sam, or turned up at a party in full Highland dress, as I saw my friend Don Harron do the other evening, I can guess at the stir he would cause. In Canada, on the contrary, it is less a mark of eccentricity than of social status. My colleague Gordon Sinclair, a third-generation Canadian, doesn't own a dinner jacket; when formal garments are required he turns up in a kilt — even on television. My fellow writer Farley Mowat wears one on almost every occasion, even though his forebears, including one premier of Ontario, emigrated to this country more than a century ago. People with scarcely a dash of Highland blood, and some with none at all, turn up in kilts on the slightest provocation. This seems to include almost everybody in Nova Scotia, which even has its own official tartan.

Like the babushka, the kilt is a symbol of our confused loyalties. When a former Polish diplomat in Canada tells a Senate committee — as he did some years ago — that his people have two loyalties, one to the new country, another to the old, no one is surprised or dismayed. One senator, Arthur Roebuck, agrees, remarking that the English in Canada also have two loyalties: " . . . we have not forgotten the culture and history of our own particular Motherland, Great Britain. In that respect, the Poles are not different from ourselves."

From the point of view of the British, that double loyalty was necessary if Canada were not to fall into the arms of you Americans. The melting pot concept, after all, is a revolutionary idea — a rejection of homeland and hence a rejection of established values. The conservative elite who ran this country wanted no part of it, since this process — the "spirit of levelling," to quote John Strachan — would have badly eroded their power base. Better to keep the newcomers compartmentalized, nearer to the bottom of the social scale.

It is hard for some of my countrymen, exposed to

your movies and literature, not to wish that we were more like you: that every Ukrainian, Swede or Italian arriving at Halifax or Toronto would become an instant Canadian, like the boys in Company B in your war movies, or the baseball players with all the foreign names who are as American as apple pie, or all those tenement kids in Hollywood's version of East Side New York. Your media have made a virtue of the melting pot. And when Canadians worry about "national unity," or the lack of it, they are really saying that we are different from you and they somehow wish we weren't. We have this habit, Sam, of seizing on the American model and believing it to be the only one.

But there is a good deal to be said for diversity. Without it, our culture would be pallid indeed. I point out to you, Sam, that the one group in your country that was not stirred into your traditional melting pot was black America. As a result, a separate culture flourishing underground has now had an enriching influence on your music, theatre, dance, sport, fashion, language. In that sense you profited accidentally from the mosaic concept.

I've already admitted that our virtual exclusion of the blacks has been our cultural loss. Our retention of Quebec's culture has been an immeasurable gain, as has our forced acceptance (because of the Quebec example) of ethnic diversity, and latterly our official support of the multicultural mosaic. Our two great waves of immigration, one before the first world war, the other following the second, changed this country out of all recognition and certainly for the better.

Actually, in spite of the furor they caused at the time, the largest group of immigrants in the first years of the century weren't Slavic peasants but American farmers. At least 600,000 crossed the border before the Great War and settled in the Canadian West. Of all the "ethnic" groups to arrive, they were the largest, the most powerful, the wealthiest and the most easily assimilated.

This mass exodus seriously alarmed many Americans. Suddenly the flow to the frontier had been reversed. But others felt it would mean the end of Canada, that at the very least the country west of Ontario would soon become part of the United States. In 1903, a writer in *Cosmopolitan* declared that "it has long seemed the part of manifest destiny that this union should come." The adventure writer James Oliver Curwood thought that "a new nation will be born in the West, formed of the very flesh and blood of the United States."

Well, in one sense a new nation was born, for western Canada, like Quebec (though to a lesser extent) is a separate state within a state. But few Canadians in those days really worried about an American takeover. The Americans who crossed the border, having sold their farms at a profit and received free homesteads on the Canadian prairies, were very much like the Americans who had poured into Upper Canada a century before. They were less interested in national loyalty than they were in making good in a rich, new land.

It was the British who were really concerned about the heavy American immigration into Canada — and with good reason. The immigrants had every reason to love the land that had enriched them; but they had no ties with the mother country. They posed no threat to Canada; but they did pose a threat to the concept of Empire. I am convinced, as others are, that the wave of national feeling that followed the first war and brought about the decline of imperial power in my country was due, in part, to the fervent Canadianism of the newly converted.

*N*ow, Sam, we must look into the whole matter of religion in Canada, for religion cannot be divorced from the mosaic. I realize that your country is no stranger to Catholic-Protestant bitterness and that we have had Roman Catholic prime ministers long before your people would accept a Roman Catholic president. In spite of that, the religious bitterness in Canada has been more manic because here it is bound up with language and race as well as with politics.

It goes back to the days before Confederation when each of the two Canadas, one French-speaking and Catholic, the other English-speaking and Protestant, was terrified that the other's culture would swallow their own. The split grew worse when separate schools for Catholics were established in the Protestant upper province, largely through the vote of the French Canadians in the lower.

This problem of schools and language has bedevilled us ever since. Do any of your people oppose the teaching of a second language in school? I doubt it. But in much of Canada, when that language is French, there has been bitter opposition. Even the appearance of the French language on breakfast cereal packages in the West has been condemned.

Now, conversely, we are faced with demands from other language groups who insist that the state support the teaching of "heritage languages" in the public schools — Ukrainian in Winnipeg, Chinese in Toronto. Canada is officially a bilingual country; it may be well on the way to becoming multilingual, except, of course, in Quebec where the babble of immigrant tongues is being officially stilled and a man can be jailed for putting up a sign in any language other than French. If that sounds spooky to you it does to me, too. It, too, is part of the essence of Canadianism, but it's not easy to explain to an outsider.

I have made the point that we are a relatively nonviolent people. However, where religion is concerned we have often been intemperate. Men have died in street brawls between Protestants and Catholics — a dozen killed in St. John's in July of 1849, for instance — tragedies that go back to the establishment, in Brockville, Upper Canada, in 1830, of the Grand Orange Lodge of British North America. These Orangemen were a bitter bunch. One of our rare rebellions became a religious war when the Métis leader, Louis Riel, a good Catholic, executed a pugnacious Orangeman, Thomas Scott. Partly as a result, the Tories, who hanged Riel, have not since that time been able to make much headway politically in the province of Quebec.

I'll never forget my arrival in New York a year ago, on March 17. As a Canadian I was only dimly aware that this was an Irish-American saturnalia; but I soon found out. The town seemed demented, the streets awash with people openly drinking Irish whiskey and tottering into Irish saloons. An extraordinary number of these people seemed to have painted themselves green. Some had green hair; some had green faces. Even the flowers in my hotel lobby were painted green. And, since all the policemen appeared to be marching in that interminable five-hour parade down Fifth Avenue, nobody seemed to give a damn that the gutters were crammed with drunken children.

As I've said at the outset, we have an Irish parade, too, in our biggest English-speaking city, although of late it has become a bit moth-eaten. But nobody paints himself orange on the Glorious Twelfth, for your Protestant Irishman is a more dour soul than his Roman compatriot.

The Irish Catholics seem to have preferred your country, Sam; the Protestants were clearly drawn to mine, for they outnumbered the Catholics two to one at the time of Confederation. I suspect this may have been partly a matter of temperature which, I shall suggest later, has something to do with temperament. To the ebullient southern Irish, our chilly northern clime must have seemed incompatible. There was also the fact that in Canada an English-speaking Catholic was close to the bottom of the social scale and far removed from the power base.

Don't you find it intriguing that in your municipal politics the Catholic Irish were dominant while in my country it was just the reverse? Tammany Hall was an Irish Catholic preserve. Toronto City Hall was run by Orangemen. Given the state of religious animosity here, they could hardly be anything else. As little as a quarter-century ago, Toronto could still elect an out-spoken pillar of the Orange Lodge as mayor. But we had two Jewish mayors before we had a Catholic.

Yet it was only at the municipal level that the Orange politicians prospered. The Irish formed the largest English-speaking group in pioneer Canada, but the Scots held the real power. Although they formed only one-fifteenth of the population in the Confederation years, the Scots controlled the fur trade, the banks, the financial houses, the major universities and, to a considerable degree, the government. For 90 per cent of the time we've been led by a prime minister of either French or Scottish extraction. If we pronounce "about" in a vaguely Gaelic fashion, it's a tribute to the Scottish influence.

The Irish were divided by history and religion, but the Scots were always single-minded — and Protestant. While the Irish brawled in the streets and taverns, the

Scots, with Gaelic zeal and Calvinistic sobriety, were running the country.

Let me introduce you to another Canadian hero, George Stephen, the first president of the CPR. His name is immortalized by a Montreal gentleman's club, a main street in Calgary and a spectacular mountain in the Rockies; but his real monument is the great railway that he financed. With other Scots, such as his frigidly aloof cousin, Donald Smith, he was part of an inter-locking directorate whose power reached into the boardrooms of the major Canadian institutions — the Bank of Montreal, the Hudson's Bay Company, McGill University and the Parliament of Canada.

See him now, at the end of his career, receiving the freedom of the city of Aberdeen where he once worked as a draper's assistant: a lean, stooped figure with a sombre hound's face, recalling his Spartan training when, as a boy of fifteen, he left school and went to work: "It was impressed upon me from my earliest years by one of the best mothers that ever lived that I must aim at being a thorough master of the work by which I had to get my living; and to be that I must con-centrate my whole energies on my work...to the exclu-sion of every other thing...."

Not for George Stephen the pursuit of happiness; no hobbies for him, with the single exception of fly fishing; no distractions. This flinty ethic, as unyielding as the Rockies themselves, has had a powerful effect on us. If we are a sober people who sometimes equate "fun" with "sin" and liquor with the devil; if we feel guilty when we succumb to distractions; if we squirrel away our money in banks at twice your per capita rate; if we are canny to the point of overcaution — some of these qualities are traceable to the Scottish influence and the Scottish example. For of all the immigrant cultures that form the Canadian mosaic, the most admired is the Scottish. Which helps explain why the wearing of the kilt, at a formal dinner, a writers' convention or even on a television panel, is considered in my country a mark of distinction and not a piece of eccentricity.

FIVE

When mercury freezes

---

*Our bracing
northern winters will preserve us from
the effeminacy which naturally steals over
the most vigorous races when under the
relaxing influence of tropical or
even generally mild and genial skies.*

GLOBE, TORONTO, 1869

*D*ear Sam:

Today is Discovery Day in my home town, the anniversary of the great gold find on Bonanza Creek, traditionally celebrated by an afternoon of sports and a harvest festival. Yes, that's right: mid-August is autumn in the Canadian north; in fact in some years there was no harvest festival because the frost had already blackened the vegetation and there was nothing to display. I call this to mind because you picked up a reference in an earlier letter to climate as an influence on the way Canadians act. Let me explain.

You will probably agree that one of the best-known Canadians of his time was the late Professor Marshall McLuhan of the University of Toronto. Remember McLuhan, the guru of the sixties, the darling of your media before he became the darling of ours? The medium, he said, was the message; but he also identified certain media in terms of temperature. In McLuhan's view, radio was a "hot" medium; television was "cool."

The analogy is fascinating. Had McLuhan not been a Canadian would he have used those symbols? Would they have sprung as easily, for instance, from the mind of a professor at UCLA or the Sorbonne? Canadians like McLuhan think in terms of climate because climate has shaped our history and affected the way we think and act. This is, after all, a country where mercury freezes in the thermometer (at 40° below celsius or Fahrenheit) — a country of winter festivals from the Whitehorse dog derby to the Quebec carnival; of parkas and toques, mukluks and moccasins; toboggans, snowmobiles and komatiks; ice-fishing, ice-boating and curling. Our great cultural rite, uniting Canadians of every creed and tongue from St. Anthony to Tofino, is Hockey Night in Canada. The Ski-doo people from Quebec keep your airport runways clear each winter; our weather — cold blasts from the Arctic — turns up regularly on your TV screens. We are a cool country, Sam. We live with snow and ice. The igloo is our one indigenous piece of architecture.

Let us visit the McCord Museum in Montreal and pore over the society portraits of William Notman, the great nineteenth-century photographer. My God, Sam, half the leading businessmen in town seem to have posed in fur coats and hats with fake snow on their shoulders and more at their ankles. Notman has even *painted* snow on the glass negatives, half obscuring his subjects in an ersatz blizzard. There is more: here is one of his greatest photographic triumphs, a composite of hundreds of snowshoers, posing in toques and sashes against a wintry background. And here is another composite in full colour of the crowning event of the Montreal social season — the Governor General's skating party.

You will be amused to learn that all this obeisance to winter irked one of your compatriots, the dynamic railway builder, William Van Horne, lured to Canada to manage the construction of the CPR. Van Horne, who needed tourists from other lands to ride his railway, was engaged in a vigorous, if largely futile, attempt to convince the world that his adopted country was, if not exactly subtropical, at least temperate. When urged to support a winter carnival in Winnipeg, he curtly turned down the request: "Ice palaces, Indians and dog trains are not popular features in our foreign advertising," he wrote. "For some inscrutable reason nearly everybody in Canada has his photograph taken in furs with salt scattered over to represent snow.... Few people in England have ever seen a Canadian picture except in winter dress. For this reason the name of Canada is almost universally associated with an Arctic climate and this idea is one of the most difficult to remove from the minds of people abroad."

Van Horne offered to contribute liberally to what he called a "shirt tail" carnival, complete with linen dusters and palm leaf fans but this facetious idea got nowhere. Canadians might protest when Kipling coined the phrase "Our Lady of the Snows" and argue that the continental interior from Last Chance Creek to Schefferville is almost tropical in July; it does no good. Deep in our hearts we know that we live in a cold country and had better make the best of it.

I wonder, Sam, if McLuhan's analogy can't be applied to nations? It seems to me there are cool nations and hot nations and that this is not entirely a matter of climate. Certainly, Italy, Spain, Greece and southern France and the other Mediterranean countries are hot — not just climatically but also emotionally. These are demonstrative peoples, openly warm, even passionate, easily provoked to laughter, tears and sometimes revolt. They live out of doors on the streets or in sidewalk cafés, filling balconies and windows, jostling one another in the cities without embarrassment, the men often arm in arm. The Scandinavians, Teutons and Anglo-Saxons to the north are less demonstrative, more phlegmatic, less openly emotional.

And so it is with us, Sam. We are cooler than you, as our people learned when your southerners invaded Upper Canada. Hot weather and passion, gunfights and race riots go together. Your mythic encounters seem to have taken place at high noon, the sun beating down on a dusty Arizona street. I find it difficult to contemplate a similar gunfight in Moose Jaw in the winter, the bitter rivals struggling vainly to shed two pairs of mitts and reach under several layers of parka for weapons so cold that the slightest touch of flesh on steel would take the skin off their thumbs.

All whimsy aside, we are very much an indoor people, a closed-door people, a diffident people because we are a northern people; and, as a pioneer country, we attracted other northern peoples — Scots, Scandinavians, Slavs, northern Irish. We maintain a polite distance from our fellow creatures, for we are not a back-slapping race: rightly or wrongly, that is how we view you Americans. Our wintry reserve cools our human enthusiasms. Maybe our recent heavy Italian immigration will leaven our crustiness but that is still in the future. As a friend of mine remarked the other day: "You ask an American how he's feeling and he cries "Great!" You ask a Canadian and he answers "Not bad," or "Pas mal."

We do not make friends as easily as you do, perhaps from a fear of being too forward. As my daughter's well-travelled Swiss landlady once remarked, she could always tell a Canadian from an American "because an American acts as if he is at home wherever he goes, a Canadian always acts as a guest."

Public displays of emotion embarrass us. Some years ago a television host, Laurier Lapierre, allowed a single tear to fall while introducing an especially touching film. It was a matter of much critical comment and I don't think he's ever quite recovered. I myself get a queasy feeling when, at your public meetings and political conventions, you all place your hands over your hearts and recite the oath of allegiance. I cannot imagine a similar group in Halifax or Vancouver or even Toronto the Good indulging in such a display of patriotism. We Canadians can't get the words of our national anthem right, possibly because they keep changing.

You Americans have an astonishing number of national patriotic songs: "God Bless America"; "It's a Grand Old Flag"; "Three Cheers for the Red, White and Blue"; "My Country 'Tis of Thee"; "Hail Columbia"; "America the Beautiful" — the list goes on and on. Since "The Maple Leaf Forever" was properly consigned to the dustbin we are left with one — though we have, in our typical fashion, inserted a few geographical references into Woody Guthrie's "This Land is Your Land," so slavishly following the American lyrics that we've even inserted a definite article before "Vancouver Island" when none is needed.

Of course, we've never had a Tin Pan Alley, which helps explain why we have no war songs of our own — nothing lasting about Dieppe or Vimy Ridge, nothing about our field artillery or our wild blue yonder. When we soldiers set off on route marches in World War Two we sang British songs from World War One: "Tipperary," "Pack Up Your Troubles," "Oh What a Lovely War."

Nor have we praised the beauty of the land in song, as you have. We have few songs like "Beautiful Ohio," "San Francisco," "New York, New York," "Chicago," "My Indiana Home," any of the myriad tunes with which you lavish praise on your country. I simply cannot imagine a popular hit praising Toronto (though there have been several spoofing it) or even Alberta.

Showbusiness isn't in our blood as it is in yours, not yet anyway. As northerners we are better teachers than entertainers. Our best films, our best radio, our best television have been the kind that instructs and informs as it entertains. The public affairs program, the documentary, the serious classical drama — these are our strengths. And, come to think of it, that's not a bad accolade. But fun for fun's sake is, by and large, beyond us, perhaps because it's seen as mildly sinful.

I'm a world's fair nut, Sam. I went twice to the New York fair of 1964-65, five times to Expo '67. I loved them both, but the difference between the two approaches to an international exposition tells us something about the differences between our two peoples.

Your fair was almost pure showbusiness. At its best it was magnificent, with the genius of Disney at its backbone. At its worst it was, well, tacky. It had all the strengths and weaknesses of an old-style carnival — lively, raucous, strongly commercial, totally individualistic, often surprising, sometimes tawdry.

I don't think our fair quite reached the finest peaks of yours, though it borrowed many of the new techniques, especially in film; but it never reached the depths either. The Canadian passion for order was dominant: even the signs had to conform to an overall design. Did you know they actually measured the decibel count throughout the grounds so that the fair wouldn't be too noisy? If an exhibitor had too many decibels he was told to bring them down — or else. The design of phone booths, lights, benches, even trash baskets was rigidly controlled. Thus, the Montreal fair had some of the silence of the Canadian north, some of the coolness of the Canadian climate, some of the authority apparent in the Canadian way of life. Peace, order and strong government at Expo '67; life, anarchy and the pursuit of fun at New York. The purpose of the Canadian exposition was to inform while entertaining. In New York, for the most part, entertainment came first.

Yet, of the two, the Montreal fair was the more successful. We believe that in Canada, because *Time* magazine said so. It had more substance, for one thing, and it was less nerve-wracking. Still, if we hadn't borrowed some of your proven showbusiness techniques, and enlarged upon them, it mightn't have been such a hit.

It seems to me, Sam, now that we are carrying this north-south analogy into the entertainment field, that one of the basic differences between us is your romanticism contrasted with our northern realism. Our earnest Film Board documentaries and our sturdy public affairs programs contrast sharply with your mythic view of America. A moment ago I told you about our failure to romanticize our cities and geographical beauty spots. The only successful hit songs I know that deal with specific Canadian communities are those of Stompin' Tom Connors, a country and western singer who specializes in Canadian subjects. They could hardly be called romantic but they are certainly down to earth. Stompin' Tom sings about a truck driver bringing a load of Prince Edward Island potatoes into Toronto on Highway 401; of the back-breaking toil of picking tobacco in Southern Ontario ("Tillsonburg, Tillsonburg, my back still aches when I hear that word"); of the "boys all getting stinko on a Sudbury Saturday Night." This is good old Canadian realism, a long way from moonlight on the Wabash.

This anti-romantic attitude is closely related to what many of us refer to as the Great Canadian Put-Down. It's no accident that some of our most successful comedy has been satire. Our longest running stage revue, *Spring Thaw*, poked mild fun for two decades at Canadian sacred cows. The successful "Saturday Night Live" television show, as well as "Second City," are largely the work of Canadians.

The put-down encompasses our reluctance to support a star system in Canada. Here again we part company with American showbusiness tradition. We tend to build up institutions rather than individuals, as Gordon Sinclair discovered in the thirties when he worked for the *Toronto Star*. Back from a globe-girdling trip that made him the most spectacular journalist in the country, he found himself relegated to a minor beat. The *Star*, in short, was bigger than Sinclair or, as his boss, H.C. Hindmarsh, told me: "There's no room for prima donnas on this paper."

This has been the attitude of the Canadian Broadcasting Corporation in sharp contrast to that of your own networks. Prima donnas can get emotional, cause trouble, spread disorder, ask for more money. They aren't "cool," and all that is very un-Canadian. Only a few CBC programs — and most are of comparatively recent vintage — bear the name of the key performer. In your country, I'll bet, "As It Happens" would have quickly become "The Barbara Frum Show." Here we have bloodless catch-all names such as "Quest," "Graphic," "The Journal," "Country Calendar," "Marketplace," "Take Thirty," "Soundtrack," "Morningside," "Variety Tonight" and so on. The inference is clear: the hosts are interchangeable and therefore comparatively faceless, like the Mounties. If they cause trouble, if they become un-cool, they can be replaced without apparent damage to the program.

The best advice I ever got was from the executive producer of my own talk show, an American named Herb Sussan. The producer, Ross McLean, was a CBC graduate with enviable credits ("Tabloid," "Close-up," "Midnight Zone"). He had several suggestions for a name — suggestions along the lines of "Backtalk" or "Talkback" or something like that. But Sussan, an NBC graduate, took me aside and said simply: "Call it the Pierre Berton Show; that way no one can fire you." To his credit, Ross agreed.

You probably think Lorne Greene is an American actor, but actually we claim him. He was our top newscaster during the war and a fine classical actor at Stratford. A while back he returned to Toronto, a local boy who had made good, and his manager held a press conference at which he introduced Lorne in this fashion:

"Ladies and gentlemen, it's a pleasure for Lorne to be back in Canada. I'm sure you'll be proud when I tell you that he has just finished three smashing personal appearances at Las Vegas. As you know, Vegas audiences are among the toughest in the world, so I'm proud to be able to tell you that in the course of three shows Lorne got not one, but *two* standing ovations!"

Whereupon a voice from the rear asked the all-Canadian question: "What went wrong the third time?"

"It was at that moment," Lorne Greene remarked later, "that I knew I was back in Canada."

It is not only the media stars that we cut down to size in our country; we also give the politicians the same treatment, as every prime minister from John A. Macdonald to Pierre Trudeau has come to realize. As I have tried to explain, Sam, we venerate institutional authority in Canada; we don't venerate the individuals who wield it. Yours is the opposite attitude: you are profoundly suspicious of government authority; but you canonize your chief executive.

The pomp and panoply that surrounds your president continues to bemuse us. That reverence does not extend north of the border. I told you that I once corralled Lester Pearson for an exclusive TV interview. Screen Gems, the American television firm whose Canadian subsidiary produced the show, was ecstatic. What a coup! The prime minister on syndicated television! His office made one stipulation only: they asked that the program be free of commercial messages, a request we readily accepted. But when the program was shipped out to the dozen or more stations that carried it, three refused to run the episode: the prime ministerial presence was not considered important enough to justify the loss of revenue.

Many of my media friends grumble about the Put-Down; I grumble about it myself from time to time. And yet, Sam, I have to admit that there is something to be said for a country that doesn't go off half-cocked when a new media star skyrockets into our ken or a man on a white horse offers to lead us to glory. We've had one rueful experience with the latter: Trudeau-mania was a very un-Canadian phenomenon. We are more comfortable with our traditional scepticism toward the cult of the personality. I should point out that Mackenzie King, our most consistently unpopular prime minister, stayed in office longer than any other. Now we have begun to regard him with a weird kind of affection.

If, in our unromantic northern fashion, we do not always venerate our heroes the way you do, it is perhaps because we realize how few real heroes there are in history. Celebrity does not a hero make; neither does politics.

It is well known, of course, that the father of your country could never tell a lie. We Canadians find it difficult to lie about the father of *our* country. To put it bluntly, he was a drunkard. And frankly, Sam, nobody in this chill and austere land really gives a damn.

SIX

The solemn
land

A large and lonely land
Under a lonely sky
Save for the friendly stars;
A land not to be wooed in a day
But by a long courting.

THOMAS SAUNDERS, 1949

*D*ear Sam:

So you quarrel with the word "austere"! You say you know a good many Canadians who *aren't* austere. True enough; but in the mass, I think, we're more austere than you are. It's not just the Scottish-Loyalist-Puritan influence, not just the climate, either; it's also the geography. The late Vincent Massey, who was pretty austere himself (he acted like a governor general even before they made him one), once remarked that "geography perhaps more than the influence of the churches, has made us puritans...."

I have to point out to you that our geography is entirely different from yours. I know you think of Canada in terms of the beautiful snow-capped Rockies; after all that's what our tourist advertising and your movies concentrate on. This has given you a romantic vision of my country: Nelson Eddy warbling away among the glittering peaks; Betty Grable and John Payne cavorting at Banff; Gene Autry singing about the blue Canadian Rockies; Tin Pan Alley praising the breeze on Lake Louise. Not too much different from the High Sierras, eh, Sam? The sun always shines on these movie mountains; when Carmen Miranda sings, it's springtime in the Rockies.

But ours is not a warm geography, like yours. Even your desert is hot; ours is ice cold. Men die quickly of thirst in yours; slowly of starvation and frostbite in ours. I'm sure that when you think of your frontier you conjure up a long line of covered wagons moving westward across the plains. But our frontier was quite different: an endless expanse of gnarled, grey rock, pocked by millions of gunmetal lakes, with twisted pines, skeletal birches and stunted black spruce bending before the wind. No covered wagon could cross it, only strong men sturdy enough to hoist a canoe on their backs or to shoulder a hundred-pound pack at the end of a tump-line.

This is the stark geographical fact of Canada. We call it the Canadian Shield and I suspect you've never heard of it; certainly no Hollywood movie has ever shown it. Yet it sprawls across half of my country, two million square miles of rocky desert, virtually uninhabitable. Its interior is trackless. The roads and railways only skirt its edges. It cannot support a market garden, let alone a farm. Only one Canadian in ten lives on the Shield, mainly in transient mining communities scattered along its outer rim.

Let me take you to the Midnight Sun Golf Tournament in Yellowknife, on the margin of the Shield where, eons ago, gold bubbled up from the earth's core to harden into veins streaking the ancient Precambrian crust. We tee off at midnight, just after sundown, and for the next nine holes we will see no blade of grass. The "greens" are made of oiled sand, the fairways are solid rock. The players, it is said, sometimes carry shotguns to drive off the ravens who swoop down and carry off the golfballs. Before our game is over, the sun is again high in the sky.

Now, Sam, suppose I take you out of the Yellowknife golf course and drop you down in the bush country in some other section of the Shield — near Reindeer Lake, Saskatchewan, say, or Thompson, Manitoba, or Sioux Lookout, Ontario, or the cottage country of Muskoka, or Quebec's Gatineau, or the interior of the Labrador plateau, more than a thousand miles away. But I doubt if you'll realize that, for the terrain has scarcely changed. For all you know you're still within shouting distance of those bizarre, grassless fairways.

For this is the overriding fact of our geography. The Shield sprawls across six provinces and most of the Northwest Territories so that from Great Slave Lake to Goose Bay the "look" is the same. Skiers in the Laurentians, vacationers in Haliburton, fly fishermen along the Saguenay River, CPR passengers skirting Lake Superior's shore, canoeists on Lake Winnipeg,

golfers at Yellowknife — all these are united by the
same geological background, the same granites,
gneisses and schists, streaked and banded, furry with
lichens, stark, austere, timeless.

Here is some of the oldest rock in the world — the
basement complex of the continent, the hard, unyielding
floor on which North America sits. But in my country
— and only in my country — the glaciers have scoured
it clean; and that is why the Canadian Shield is unique.
In tens of thousands of little armoured hollows and
furrows scooped out of the earth's crust by the advancing ice sheets, the water sits, unable to flow this
way or that because the erosion pattern has long since
been destroyed. Wilderness Canada is a land of little
lakes; no one has counted them all or set out to cross the
Shield from Hudson Bay to Coppermine and back
since Samuel Hearne made that five-thousand-mile
journey on foot — two centuries ago. Nor has the land
that Hearne traversed changed or been changed since
that day.

We are a Shield people, Sam, a wilderness people.
Every city-dweller from St. John's to Victoria is within
a few hours' drive of lake, mountains or Precambrian
rock. The Shield unites us, even though most of us have
glimpsed it only from a train window, a cottage porch,
a ski slope or a canoe. Its mystique affects us all. Our
great epic poet, Ned Pratt, likened the grim land north
of Lake Superior to a sleeping reptile, "a hybrid that
myths might have conceived . . . too old for death, too
old for life." Its presence creeps through our literature

and dominates our great school of landscape paintings. In the 1920s, the Group of Seven captured the Shield in all its moods, and through these canvasses, Canadians began to see an awesome kind of beauty in the Shield's mammillated cones, dark escarpments and wind-ravaged pines.

If there is terror in the Shield there is also grandeur; not the grandeur of Monument Valley or the Grand Canyon but something peculiarly Canadian — ridge after ridge of rumpled granite stretching for thousands of miles from the Great Lakes to the Arctic, imprisoning unnumbered serpentine lakes.

J.E.H. Macdonald's famous painting tells the story. "The Solemn Land" he called it. That title might stand for my country, Sam; for if we are a solemn people, it is partly because the Shield and the wilderness bear down upon us, a crushing weight, squeezing us like toothpaste along the borders of your country.

On the map Canada looks square; in reality we are another Chile, with nine-tenths of our people living within two hundred miles of your border, an archipelago of population islands walled off from each other by the terrifying obstacles of Precambrian rock, muskeg, mountain barriers, storm-tossed waters.

Muskeg — that's another typically Canadian word. We have 500,000 square miles of it, more than any other country in the world. As our early railroad builders learned, these vast spongy half-frozen bogs of moss, water, peat and slime can gobble an entire locomotive at a single gulp, not to mention a mile of track and a quarter-million yards of gravel. Perhaps that explains why, if your frontier epics have to do with the taming of the Indians, ours are concerned with the taming of the land.

*W*e have always had a love-hate relationship with the Shield, Sam. It has helped give us a common identity but it has also acted as a dam, thwarting western expansion. At the time of Confederation we were a small, constricted nation, imprisoned within the confines of the St. Lawrence lowlands — a narrow country of narrow roads, narrow streets and, some would say, of narrow minds. One thousand miles of broken rock and reeking muskegs stood between the settled nation and the great plains. People in those days talked of the prairie country as we today might talk of Tibet; it was fascinating but unreachable.

It's time I introduced you to a young British officer, William Francis Butler, a romantic young man with a long face and long, tight side whiskers to match. It is October 1872, the frost already thick on the yellowed grass of the prairie. But winter holds no terrors for this ambitious and impulsive young subaltern who is setting off, with a single guide, on a four-thousand-mile odyssey across what he will call "that great, boundless solitary waste of verdure," from the Red River to the foot of the Rockies and back.

The result is a bestseller whose title, *The Great*

Lone Land, puts a new phrase into the language. Butler's eloquent descriptions of the night-shadowed prairie, the immensity of the ocean of grass, the infinite silence of nature, captured the imagination of his readers. But though the literate public gobbled up his haunting narrative, there was nothing the average person could do about it. The Shield was in the way; even Butler had not crossed it.

The country was full of free spirits in those days, yearning to follow a moving frontier. We lost them, Sam — lost some of our most adventurous souls at a time we could ill afford it. Since only the hardiest fur traders could traverse the Shield, the rest went south and, though a few trickled north again to the Red River, most followed the covered wagons to the American west. At this point, one quarter of all Canadians were living on your side of the border. These included a tavernkeeper from Toronto Township named Cody whose son, William, rose to fame on your frontier as Buffalo Bill. In those days, far-off fields really *were* greener.

So we lost many of our boldest and most independent spirits. On the other hand, the frustrating presence of the Precambrian country made possible a more stable kind of Canadian frontier. In the United States, the settlers moved west ahead of the law. But when ours finally reached the prairies, thanks to the new railway, the law was already in place. Thus, in an odd way, the presence of this bizarre wasteland is one of the reasons why our frontier history is comparatively bloodless.

I have said that the Shield united us, giving us a common landscape, unique in the world. But it can also be blamed for the bitter schism between East and West.

To ensure an all-Canadian railway — one that would span that thousand-mile desert on its way to the Pacific — John A. Macdonald was forced into a Faustian bargain with George Stephen. Like everybody else in those days, Stephen thought the only sensible route west was *around* the Shield. That would mean moving it south in a great arc, through American territory.

Macdonald wouldn't have it. And so, to get what he wanted, knowing in his heart that he was igniting the slow fuse of prairie disaffection, he was forced to acccpt the CPR's ultimatum. Stephen wanted a monopoly and Macdonald agreed: no other Canadian line could be built within fifteen miles of the border for the next twenty years.

Sam, it's difficult for anybody not raised in western Canada to understand the bitter antipathy of prairie folk to the Canadian Pacific Railway. In the early days it bordered on the pathological. You can catch the flavour of it in a letter Clifford Sifton wrote to a Winnipeg friend in 1897. As Minister of the Interior, Sifton was the most powerful westerner in the government. Now he was decrying the nomination of a weak candidate in a Winnipeg by-election:

"I personally know he is not in a position to be a candidate," Sifton wrote. "Disclosures will be made during the campaign which will cause him to be defeated. He is at present in the employ of the Canadian Pacific Railway Company, and, as you know, that would be fatal to his candidature.... Just fancy yourself in the middle of an election campaign having a charge made on the platform that your candidate was an employee of the Canadian Pacific Railway. The probability is that he would lose his deposit...."

The hated monopoly clause had long since been scrapped, but in the West, being allied with the CPR was still seen as close to treason. Why? Why this bitter hatred of the very railway that opened the country and without which the prairies would remain a limitless ocean of waist-high buffalo grass?

Let me try to explain it by introducing you to another Canadian, one of those free spirits who could not stand being cooped up in pre-Confederation Canada and so, at the age of sixteen, left his native Sorel to become the best-known trader in Minnesota territory and, eventually, the mayor of St. Paul. Now, in 1875, Norman Kittson is in his mid-sixties, a gaunt, patriarchal figure with a long white beard and a weathered face. He runs the Kittson steamboat line between St. Paul and Winnipeg. It's a monopoly and he charges the earth. The Manitoba merchants are so incensed at Kittson's outrageous freight rates that they determine to give him some competition. They build two rival steamboats, a rate war follows and prices tumble — but not for long.

The indomitable Kittson, in his creaky stern-wheeler, *International*, "a perfect marvel of patchwork," lurks round a bend until the newly launched

Manitoba puffs into view. Then under full steam he charges her broadside. *Crash!* Sounds of wood splintering, steam hissing, water gurgling as the *Manitoba*, cargo and all, slowly sinks below the muddy surface of the Red. Now the Manitoba merchants are in retreat — and there's more trouble ahead.

Kittson is in cahoots with another former Canadian, also lured from his home in Rockwood, Ontario, at the age of eighteen by a thirst for adventure that his own, narrow country could not slake. This is James J. Hill, "Big Jim," the one-eyed St. Paul coal-dealer who will become the greatest American railroad entrepreneur. Hill, along with Donald Smith, the future Lord Strathcona, fronting for the Hudson's Bay Company, is Kittson's silent partner. Hill has no trouble greasing the palms of the customs men at the border so that, while one steamboat is being raised from the bottom of the Red River the other is being held up indefinitely by red tape.

In the face of this spirited opposition, the Manitoba merchants call it quits and the freight rates soar — so high, it is said, that a steamboat load of goods can be shipped the entire length of the Mississippi for half the price charged by the Kittson monopoly for a three-hundred-mile-journey over slack water.

I have told this story at some length because it was the hated Kittson group — Kittson, Hill, Smith and Smith's cousin, George Stephen — who dominated the syndicate that forced Macdonald to give them a new transportation monopoly just five years after these incidents occurred.

This meant the CPR in the West could charge what the traffic would bear. It also meant that no westerner could build a rival railway to the border to compete for the lucrative American trade. And, since railways were at the core of western development and western prosperity, the West was understandably embittered — first at what was viewed as an American syndicate, later an Eastern monopoly, and finally the central government itself. For the CPR stood as the symbol of an official policy, which saw the West as a huge granary supplying the East with food while purchasing, at inflated prices, the necessary manufactured goods and farm machinery from the East.

Thus, western Canadians have seen themselves as "hewers of wood and drawers of water" (to use another classic Canadian phrase) for the moneyed interests of Central Canada. And so the Shield, like the Cordilleran spine of British Columbia and the Gulf of St. Lawrence, is a psychological as much as a physical barrier: one that helps perpetuate the tensions that make us different from you.

We are a resource country, Sam. Geography has made us so. There is no use hiding the fact that the bitterness westerners feel for Central Canada has its shadowy counterpart in the attitude of many Canadian nationalists toward your country. A glance at our trade balance shows that we have all been hewers of wood and drawers of water. If we have benefitted in the short term — selling off our raw materials, our crude oil, our pulpwood, our wheat for boom prices — these gains may well have been offset by the export of another commodity: jobs. Somebody else is paid good wages for processing our resources. This is the Great Canadian Dilemma, one of the matters we argue about, one of the things we Canadians have in common — like getting drunk on Grey Cup Night, or hating Toronto or, on a summer's evening, sitting out on those old, cracked rocks by the lake, listening to the ghostly laughter of the loon.

*W*e are coming to the end of this long screed, Sam. I had thought at the outset that I could distill the essence of my country into a few pithy paragraphs. That has not been possible, as you have perhaps come to realize, for the differences between us are both subtle and complex. That is why Canadians are often tongue-tied when asked to explain, in a sentence or two, how we differ. We know we're not the same but we can't express it succinctly; I doubt if anybody can. Then, too, we are a taciturn lot, being northerners. It embarrasses us, I think, to love our country out loud. Yet it may well be that love of country is what really holds us together.

For we are learning to love it perhaps because for the first time we see its future threatened. The prospect of divorce has made our bones rattle, and now we are forced to ask ourselves: do we really want to lose what we have built?

Our love affair with Canada has been long and slow, never a sudden infatuation. We are a wilderness nation; it has not been easy to come to terms with a harsh environment. Geography has been our enemy more often than it has been our friend. As Margaret Atwood, one of our best poets and critics, has explained, our literature has been obsessed with the problem of survival.

But love at first sight is a slick short story writer's myth and, as I have tried to show, we are not romantics. Sudden romances have a habit of burning out. So we have come to terms with the tensions that obsess us, slowly and cautiously in the Canadian fashion. I think we are beginning to understand that these tensions will not go away, that we must learn to live with them, adapt to them and survive them, as we have survived our appalling geography. This is part of being Canadian.

It has occurred to me recently, that in spite of our propensity for general disengagement, we are now for the first time beginning to see our country whole, in the physical sense. For decades we were like blind men, familiar with only one part of the elephant. Just as in the days before the railway only a handful could visit the West, so in the days before the automobile and the airplane only a handful could explore the Cabot Trail or the Malahat. Just as our painters electrified the country in the 1920s by showing for the first time the glory of the Canadian Shield and the Canadian north, so in our own time have we begun to sense the beauty and the mystique of the land through television.

You had the movies, Sam, to show off your country. New York, Chicago, Philadelphia, St. Louis, San Francisco were all glamorized by Hollywood. But nobody in Vancouver ever saw Toronto or Halifax on the screens of the twenties, thirties or forties. Your history and geography, often mythologized and prettified, were made familiar to millions by hundreds of major films. But no Hollywood movie ever showed our prairies. *North West Mounted Police* was shot in California; *Saskatchewan* was made in the Rockies. The majority of Canadians in those years were more familiar with the bayous of Louisiana, the blue grass of Kentucky, the hill country of Tennessee and the Arizona desert than they were with the Bay of Fundy's tidal bore, the red roads of Prince Edward Island or the fiords of British Columbia.

That has changed. Even as we threaten to fly apart, the love of the land holds us together. It is *our* land, Sam, nobody else's; and, as we are beginning to realize, it is like no other. I should like to show it to you, in all its beauty and all its terror, but that would take a lifetime. Perhaps, though, we can make a swift tour by air, hitting a few of the high spots that, I am certain, are unknown to you and only now becoming known to my own people.

Let us begin by hovering over that vast natural trough we call the Rocky Mountain Trench, the most continuous gap in the continent that stretches northwest from the British Columbia border, eleven hundred miles into the Yukon. Five great rivers and now a manmade lake lie on its floor, but we cannot linger here for, as we reach the Yukon border, the limestone canyons, hot springs and waterfalls of the Nahanni country beckon. Here is a mile-deep gorge and a cataract twice as high as Niagara and, to the east, beyond the Mackenzie mountains, two great freshwater seas, the largest lakes in the world, one of them, Great Bear, so cold that plankton cannot live in its waters.

North now to the Arctic's rim and the delta of the Mackenzie River, an immense natural sponge, six thousand square miles of it, punctured by a million ponds and veined by a network of muddy, wriggling channels. There seems no end to this watery labyrinth, stretching off into the haze of the horizon, glinting upwards in the summer midnight like a gigantic broken mirror. But we must leave it and swoop south and east across the vast cold desert we call the Barren Ground.

There it is below us, the treeless tundra, majestic in its monotony. Here lies the evidence of the last great ice sheet that smothered half a continent: prodigious rocks, house-size, bulldozed hundreds of miles by the advancing glaciers; long drumlin lines — the clawmarks of the monster; snakelike ridges known as eskers, the remains of rivers flowing beneath a mile-thick wall of ice. The musk-oxen scamper in tight groups across the shattered rocks of a moraine directly below; the caribou ebb and flow in dark currents. Beautiful haunting country, Sam — and deadly. Not far from those white sand beaches in the Thelon country —

whiter than the beaches of Waikiki — men have died by inches of hunger.

We have reached Fort Churchill, Canada's farthest north grain port on the bleak margin of Hudson Bay, the great continental sea that acts as the country's thermostat. It is June. Below us the pack ice is breaking up, the sun catching the gleam of black water showing through the slushy channels. The Canadian spring is creeping north.

We have come more than a thousand miles from the Mackenzie delta and now we must fly another thousand miles northeast toward Baffin, the greatest of our islands, the fourth-largest in the world, twice the size of New Zealand. Here is a formidable land of jagged bluc mountains, long swirling glaciers and fingers of frozen ocean. On this one island, there are sixteen thousand miles of crinkled coastline, including the longest fiord in the world, Admiralty Inlet. There it is, the cliffs rising a thousand feet sheer from the sea, the island's backbone mantled by the Barnes ice cap, a relic of the Pleistocene Age, still a quarter of a mile thick.

We are turning south, toward home. The low, withered tip of the island is below us, the surface like freshly stirred porridge, as we head out across Hudson Strait, that deep ocean trough gouged out by a mile-thick river of ice, squeezing out of Hudson Bay. We have a long way yet to go; Ottawa is twelve hundred miles due south.

We cross the mouth of Ungava Bay. Just below us we can see the thousand-foot cliffs of Akpotak Island rising out of the sea, a dark triangle, thirty miles long, unreachable by any human because its edges are perpendicular with the ocean. Beyond lies the world's largest crater, created four thousand years ago by a meteor that gouged out ten billion tons of rock in a blast that makes the Hiroshima explosion seem like a firecracker.

Now we are crossing the interior Labrador plateau, with the Torngat Mountains on our left, which the Eskimos call "evil spirits." They are not really mountains but prodigious folds of rock, boiling out of the ocean, horn-shaped or saw-toothed. I have described the Labrador interior elsewhere as "an unearthly world, half fairyland, half purgatory" — a phrase that might easily cover most of the uninhabited country we have encountered. This is a land of boiling rivers, harsh canyons, camel-backed mountains and cliffs that seem to have been split in twain by a gigantic cleaver. But now, with the arches forming a green mist in the valleys and a thousand waterfalls dropping in lacy cascades from the granite scarps, the face of Labrador smiles. The soil below us glimmers redly, for much of this land is pure rust, holding a trove of iron treasure now being gouged out and transported to the sea by the most spectacular of all railways — the Iron Ore Express that knifes and bores its way through the natural bastion of the Laurentian Scarp.

The Gulf of St. Lawrence lies ahead and, to the west, the mouth of the long water highway that leads to the heart of the continent and has, as its continuation, the lakes and the horizontal rivers that lead across the prairies and trickle through the mountain passes to give Canada its shape and its reason for being. For we are a nation of canoeists, and have been since the earliest days, paddling our way up the St. Lawrence, across the lakes, over the portages of the Shield, west along the North Saskatchewan through the Yellowhead gap and thence southwest by the Columbia and the Fraser rivers to the sea. When somebody asks you how Canada could exist as a horizontal country with its plains and mountains running vertically, tell him about the paddlers, Sam.

Three things will have struck you in the course of this exhausting semi-circular tour of the Canadian wilderness: vast distances, colossal size and, above all, the absence of human beings and human scale. Dwarfed by nature, we Canadians have every reason to feel like lesser creatures in a Brobdingnagian world. Few have seen the cliffs of Baffin or the eskers of the tundra but we all live cheek by jowl with the wilderness; and all of us, I think, *feel* the empty and awesome presence of the North. If we are not as cocky as we might wish to be, if we are more sober than those who live by placid, sunlit waters, it is partly because of an uncanny environment that beckons even as it repels, seductive in its beauty, fearsome in its splendour.

So we have come to the end of our journey, Sam, and I hope now, when you visit my country, there will be fewer questions to ask about this queer, complicated nation. If I have been sweeping in my generalizations,

I apologize; you are right when you say that all Canadians are not as sober, austere or chilly as I have made out. I believe these to be national characteristics but there are numberless exceptions; and, as our ethnic make-up changes, as our cities grow larger and our small towns diminish, as our ancestral memories recede, we, too, will metamorphize. It's happened in my own time.

We are still too strait-laced to sell beer in Toronto delis but I can remember the day when sidewalk saloons were also banned in the Queen City because the authorities believed, in their Puritan fashion, that the patrons, inebriated to the point of imbecility, would tumble into the gutters to be mashed by passing autos. Now we have dozens of these outdoor bistros and as yet no innocent bystander has suffered the loss of life or limb. This very summer, in an astonishing breakthrough, the Upper Canadian government has actually launched a courageous experiment by allowing the limited sale of beer in three selected sports stadiums. We are told, further, that if the expected saturnalia does not result, if the fans do not totter down the aisles and collapse on the baseball diamond sodden with drink, then, in good time, the policy may be extended.

So you see, we *are* changing, as you suggested in your last letter, but quietly, a step at a time, in our own fashion.

Can I make you understand, even as I poke mild fun at certain of our national characteristics that, in bulk, I accept them and even applaud them? When I compare our two peoples I do not intend to make invidious comparisons, only to demonstrate that, sometimes for better and sometimes for worse, we have our own distinct identity and our own way of doing things and that part of that identity is our tendency to constant self-examination.

This is not the first time I've compared our differing characters. On occasion I venture across the border to attempt that task, often, I fear, with indifferent results. It's not easy to explain to you Americans that we're not only different but that we also *like* being different and that that implies no disrespect for you.

I once laid out some of these theories in a speech to an audience in upstate New York, at the end of which a dear old lady came forward, took me by the arm and, with a fervency that was disarming, made me realize that nothing I had said had made much impact.

"But we *love* you Canadians," she said in a hurt voice. "We just *love* you!" — as if that made everything all right.

But you see, old friend, it's not your love we want; it's your understanding. And that, I guess, we can never have until we understand ourselves.

BOOKS BY PIERRE BERTON

The Royal Family
The Mysterious North
Klondike
Just Add Water and Stir
Adventures of a Columnist
Fast, Fast, Fast Relief
The Big Sell
The Comfortable Pew
The Cool, Crazy, Committed World of the Sixties
The Smug Minority
The National Dream
The Last Spike
Drifting Home
Hollywood's Canada
My Country
The Dionne Years
The Wild Frontier
The Invasion of Canada
Flames Across the Border
Why We Act Like Canadians
The Promised Land
Vimy

PICTURE BOOKS
The New City (*with Henri Rossier*)
Remember Yesterday
The Great Railway
The Klondike Quest

ANTHOLOGIES
Great Canadians
Pierre & Janet Berton's Canadian Food Guide
Historic Headlines

FOR YOUNGER READERS
The Golden Trail
The Secret World of Og

FICTION
Masquerade (*pseudonym Lisa Kroniuk*)